A HISTORY OF ESSEX

The Norman Keep of the de Veres, Earls of Oxford, dominates the town of Castle Hedingham

THE DARWEN COUNTY HISTORY SERIES

A History of Essex

A. C. EDWARDS

Drawings by Carolyn Lockwood

PHILLIMORE

First published 1958
Fourth edition 1978
by

PHILLIMORE & CO. LTD.,
London and Chichester

Head Office: Shopwyke Hall,
Chichester, Sussex, England

ISBN 0 85033 280 X

Printed in England by
UNWIN BROTHERS, LTD.,
at the Gresham Press, Old Woking, Surrey

and bound by
THE NEWDIGATE PRESS LTD.,
at Book House, Dorking, Surrey

Contents

	List of Maps	6
	List of Plates	7
	Acknowledgements	9
	Preface—The Components of Essex History	11
I	Prehistoric and Roman Essex	14
II	The Kingdom of the East Saxons	20
III	The Middle Ages: The Church in Essex	25
IV	The Middle Ages: The Land and the People	34
V	Ancient Borough, Markets and Fairs	40
VI	The Reformation and its Consequences	50
VII	The Siege of Colchester	57
VIII	The Homes of Essex	61
IX	Old-established Essex Grammar Schools	72
X	Georgian Essex	75
XI	Parliamentary Representation	81
XII	Early Roads and Improved Waterways	85
XIII	The Coming of the Railway	89
XIV	The Seaboard of Essex	93
XV	The Latest Age	96
XVI	A Select Dictionary of Essex Biography	105
	Index	125

Maps

1.	Roman Essex	17
2.	Essex of the Saxons	21
3.	Essex parish churches	26
4.	Some features of Domesday Essex	35
5.	Ancient boroughs, markets and fairs	41
6.	Religious houses of Essex	51
7.	Essex homes	63
8.	Parliamentary representation	83
9.	The turnpike roads of Essex	87
10.	Principal railways of Essex	91
11.	Present day Essex in London	101

List of Illustrations

	Hedingham Castle Keep (colour)	*frontispiece*
1.	Balkerne Gate, Colchester	*facing page* 16
2.	Bartlow Hills, Ashdon	16
3.	St. Peter's-on-the-Wall, Bradwell-on-Sea	17
4.	Greensted Church	17
5.	Deed settling dispute between Barking Abbey and the Knights of St. John	32
6.	Brass of Earl and Countess of Essex	33
7.	Virgin and Child, Great Canfield (colour)	40
8.	St. Osyth's Abbey	*between pages* 40-41
9.	Pleshey Castle	40-41
10.	Map of Housham Hall, Matching	40-41
11.	Prior's Hall Barn, Widdington	40-41
12.	Walker's map of Chelmsford, 1591 (colour)	*facing page* 41
13.	Maldon	64
14.	Thaxted	64
15.	Deane's map of Colchester, 1748 ..	*between pages* 64-65
16.	Harwich in the Reign of Queen Anne	*facing page* 65
17.	Barking	65
18.	Romford	80
19.	Dedham	80
20.	Siege of Colchester	*between pages* 80-81
21.	St. Clere's Hall, St. Osyth	*facing page* 81
22.	Barley Barn, Cressing	81
23.	Plan of Ingatestone Hall, 1805	96
24.	Bower Hall, Steeple Bumpstead	*between pages* 96-97
25.	Audley End	96-97
26.	Thorndon Hall	96-97
27.	Brass of Archbishop Harsnett	*facing page* 97
28.	Mr. Emblin's Academy, Leyton	112
29.	Fairlop Fair	112
30.	Map of South-west Essex, 1777, by Chapman and Andre .. .. *between pages* 112-113	

31.	Southend	*facing page* 113
32.	Leigh-on-Sea	113
33.	Chappel Viaduct	120
34.	J. J. Mechi's Farm, Tiptree	120
35.	Stansted Airport .. .. *between pages*	120-121
36.	M.11 Motorway	120-121
37.	Broad Walk, Harlow	120-121
38.	Bradwell Power Station	120-121
39.	Virgin and Child and the Risen Christ, Lambourne	*facing page* 121

Acknowledgements

Acknowledgments are, inevitably, almost the last part of a book to be written. By then the author is feeling a little jaded; and for weeks, maybe months, he has become increasingly conscious of his growing debt to others and terrified lest he should omit somebody.

Two debts have been inherited from the past and must be re-acknowledged: first, to K. J. Lace, the former Essex County Librarian who so kindly suggested my name to Lord Darwen, then managing director of Darwen Finlayson, Ltd.; the second is to Lord Darwen himself, who treated me with great patience and forbearance. *Essex* was one of the early books in the original series, but shortly before Phillimore Ltd. took over, Lord Darwen introduced a new style and format, and these have been continued by Phillimore, who have happily named the series The Darwen County Histories. This revised, enlarged and updated *Essex* now appears in the new format, and it has brought me into debt to many more people.

My friends in the Essex Record Office, some of them new, some of them former colleagues, have been most helpful. Ken Newton, the County Archivist, has given sound advice and has most generously allowed me to use many of the photographs from the Record Office collections; I am also grateful to Nelson Hammond and Jon Nutton, his colleagues in the photographic department. Nancy Briggs, Supervisor of the Students' Room, has read the manuscript and proofs; she has made many helpful suggestions and has steered me away from a number of pitfalls. John Booker, Senior Assistant Archivist, has readily given me the benefit of his wide knowledge of local industrial history and, particularly, of turnpike roads in Essex.

My debt to Ron Bates, an old friend and a former colleague in the Education Department, has accumulated over the years and is now greater still; his help on photographic matters has been invaluable.

I am very grateful to many others who have patiently and readily given me sensible answers to many questions—to Mike Wadhams, Peter Came, Bob Wood, Ronald Bond, S. T. Brennan, B. A. Barker, D. A. Glading, D. E. Dines, Warwick Rodwell, and Kevin Bruce. Peter Dalby has skilfully re-drawn the maps, and Mrs. Beryl Tyler has typed the book from a manuscript which has not always been a model of calligraphy. I am equally grateful to another good friend, Walter Drews, Principal of Wansfell College, for the photo of the M11 motorway;

to the Harlow Development Corporation for the view of the High; and to the Central Electricity Generating Board for the photograph of Bradwell Power Station, taken by Kevin Bruce. The prints of Pleshey and St. Osyth were supplied by the University of Cambridge's Committee for Aerial Photography, and Dr. J. K. S. St. Joseph. All other illustrations came from the Essex Record Office Collections, some from prints by the office photographic staff, some from photos by the County Visual Aids Service.

Finally, I offer my sincere thanks to Noel Osborne, the Editorial Director of Phillimore; he has been most helpful, and working with him has been a great pleasure.

Preface: The Components of Essex History

A genial wit, an Essex man born and bred, has been known to gaze sternly at his audience and begin his lecture with the words, 'Essex is NOT flat and uninteresting; Essex is slightly undulating and uninteresting'. This may not be one of his better witticisms, but but it effectively impales that most persistent of libels and slanders. Essex is NOT flat—try walking briskly up Market Hill, Maldon! As for its *interest,* this lies in the eye and mind of the beholder. For those who delight in seeking to interpret the successive layers of handwriting scratched by man on the surface of the county, there is more than enough for a lifetime of absorbing interest, a plenitude of scripts, ranging from the sweet hand of the Romans to the fading calligraphy of a Capability Brown and the obscene *graffiti* of an unbridled developer.

The physical surface of the county can be gauged, of course, from a large-scale physical map, but it has to be walked or cycled to be fully appreciated. Most of the high land is in the north and west, and not much of this is above the 350ft. contour line. In the extreme north-west are two little patches above 450ft., and the highest point, at Langley, is 458ft. But the hilliness is also widespread. In mid-Essex, the Danbury-Little Baddow high land only just tops 350ft., but from Danbury, looking southwards, the view is extensive and impressive. The Langdon Hills, right in the south and not four miles from the Thames, rise to 387ft. Even in the rising ground bordering the marshes of the Dengie peninsula, where the highest point is only 126ft., there are two stretches of road where the gradient is greater than one in nine. The hilliness is further enhanced by the river valleys. They are *old* rivers; in their upper reaches there are no gorges, but they have steadily eroded away the land so that they are now flanked by fairly steep sides which add considerably to the diversity of the landscape.

These rivers, with their tidal estuaries and the North Sea into which they flow, have contributed vastly to the history of the county. They were the ways by which the invaders came, past the remote coastal marshes and deep into Essex. And where invaders could penetrate, trade could follow, and eventually this trade became a two-way flow. All too little is known about early trade and transport, but it is certain that the waterways of Essex were used more extensively in the past than they are today.

The surface geology of the county is fairly complicated, but may be told in simple terms: chalk in the north-west and in the extreme south; chalky boulder clay spreading south-eastwards from the north-west; London Clay to the south-east; sands and gravel in the south-west. The chalky boulder clay provided rich soil for wheat; thus it is not surprising that the early East Saxon settlements ran across the centre and north-centre of the county, and that this remained the most populous area until modern times. In the past, London Clay meant oats and grazing with rich marshland pasture fairly near at hand. In the south-west on the poorer soil, the Forest of Essex formed a barrier between the county and the capital, but was pierced by the Great Essex Road, running north-east and south-west through the county like a spit, and running mainly *across* the river valleys.

It could be said, too, that the field patterns were determined by geology. The rich boulder clay land of central Essex is an area of ancient enclosure into fairly small fields of chunky shapes, enclosed well before written records became common. Maybe, in some parts of this area the enclosure was even earlier, inherited by the East Saxons from the Romans or, perhaps, even prehistoric settlers. The open-field strip cultivation lingered on in the extreme west and north, and finally died out, little more than a century ago, on the chalk uplands of the extreme north-west.

Again, geology affected the building history of the county sufficiently to warrant a long chapter in this book: the lack of good building stone; the use of inferior and less tractable stone; the inevitable reliance on timber and brick; the considerable ingenuity engendered in the use of these materials, an ingenuity which produced aesthetically pleasing churches, houses and barns.

All the considerations stated so far are topographical—considerations much neglected before the rise of Hoskins, that most original and least honoured of all modern historians. But Essex is rich, too, in materials for the orthodox archaeologist, the 'dirt' archaeologist, the delver. The study of archaeology as a whole and the application of scientific techniques to it have grown enormously in the middle decades of this century, and it is heartening to see it flourishing so vigorously in Essex. The main danger still lies in lack of time and resources to record threatened sites. Destruction of sites may be inevitable and is always regrettable; destruction of evidence before it can be recorded is a sin against history and civilisation.

As for written evidence, Essex is in an enviable position. Most of it is now in the Essex Record Office and is thoroughly catalogued and indexed. The policy of the Record Office has always been outgoing —to make the original manuscript evidence available to *all,* not to a privileged coterie, and to go even further by actively encouraging research at all levels. It is a policy which aroused some disapproval at first, but it has been widely copied and this is the sincerest form of flattery. It should be added that the *printed* word is also an essential tool and, here, the county library and other library authorities within the geographical county have provided an invaluable service.

Topography, geology, archaeology, documents, books—these are the main components of local history, and in Essex the components are plentiful and readily available. But availability does not fully explain the widespread and growing interest in local history. There is no doubt that this growing interest exists; at some points it can be *measured,* for example, by the students' room statistics at the Essex Record Office; at other points it can simply be *seen*—go to Finchingfield on a summer week-end and try to count the parked cars! Maybe it is a sympton of decay and decline—a turning to the past to escape the unpleasant realities of a pinchbeck present. Maybe it is a healthy sign—a desire in man to find out exactly how his ancestors and his environment have made him what he is. Anyhow, it is *there*, and in Essex it draws and holds an ever-increasing number. Possibly Norden had the nub of it nearly 400 years ago—'This shire is most fat, fruitful and full of profitable things'.

I Prehistoric and Roman Essex

*Roman Centurion,
Colchester*

Long before the sea flooded the low-lying land which once lay between Britain and the Continent, the area now known as Essex was occupied by the people of the Old Stone Age. Traces of these nomadic hunters have been found on the coast near Clacton, along river valleys and in the south-east of the county. Many thousands of years later, about the time that Britain became an island, men of the Middle Stone Age, more skilled in fashioning weapons and implements of flint, settled in the Colne valley and at Hullbridge. About the same time, great oak forests spread over the Essex claylands, making it difficult for all later invaders from the Continent to move inland from their settlements along the coast and the north side of the Thames. The only ways open to them were the corridors formed by river valleys, and here they were able to make their homes on the waterside terraces of well-drained gravel. The people of the New Stone Age settled on the coast of the Tendring Hundred, in the Rochford Hundred, and in the Lea valley. Their weapons and implements of flint were smoothly polished and given sharp edges by grinding; one of their 'factories' for making them has been found at Walton-on-the-Naze.

From about 1800 B.C. there were many groups of fresh settlers, all of whom knew how to make weapons, implements and ornaments of bronze. The earliest of these, known as 'Beaker' men from the shape of their pottery, settled in the Clacton area and on the north bank of the Thames. A later group who reached the Thames between 1000 and 750 B.C. were lakeside dwellers from the Alps; one of their *crannogs* or pile-dwellings has been found near Southchurch.

There is still a great deal to be discovered about early settlers in Essex. Archaeologists have been finding remains in the interior of the Tendring Hundred, where the soil is light and there were probably no dense forests in prehistoric times. More finds have been made on the foreshores of Essex, for the coastline has sunk several feet in the last 2,000 years. One off-shore track has always been known. This is the Broomway from Great Wakering to Foulness, running parallel to the coast and about half a mile away from it. This ancient road was used once again in 1953, for it was the only way by which people and cattle could be taken to safety from Foulness during the disastrous floods.

The earliest Celts of the Iron Age, the *Trinovantes*, settled in many parts of Essex. Like the peoples of the Bronze Age, they were peaceful

14

farmers, and they were left undisturbed for nearly four centuries, for the next wave of invaders from the Continent, the fierce La Tene folk, did not spread as far eastwards as Essex. About 75 B.C., or earlier, other warlike Belgic tribes began to arrive in Britain. They were skilled metal-workers and enamellers; their pottery was wheel-made, and with their heavy ploughs they were better able than earlier people to cultivate the claylands. They soon spread from Kent to north Hertfordshire, passing up the Lea valley and constantly harrying the peaceful *Trinovantes,* who were forced to take refuge in their hill-forts on the Epping ridge. When Julius Caesar came to Britain for the second time, in 54 B.C., he invaded the area now called Hertfordshire, defeated the *Belgae*, and forced them to promise to leave the *Trinovantes* alone. The *Belgae* were too thrusting, however, to be kept out for long. Some tribes came over from Kent and settled in the south of the county. Then, about A.D. 10, Cunobelin, the leader of the Hertfordshire *Belgae,* descended on Essex. There, on a plateau of gravel between the Roman River and the Colne, he made an important settlement and protected it on the exposed west and south-west by vast earthworks. At the northern tip of this plateau, where there was a ford at the highwater point of the Colne, he built his capital, Camulodunum, the 'Stronghold of Camulus', the war-god. Here for 30 years, Cunobelin, the Cymbeline of Shakespeare's play, ruled prosperously. He had his own mint, his own potteries, his own metal-workers and corn merchants; and the remains of the red brick-earth, similar to that found in the 'Red Hills' on the Essex coast, show that he had his own saltpans. He exported gold, silver, iron, cattle, greyhounds, slaves, and, above all, corn, to the Roman markets. Among his imports were wine, brooches and other ornaments and pottery of the finest quality.

Shortly after Cunobelin died, the Emperor Claudius decided to invade Britain. In A.D. 43 he sent an army of about 50,000 under Aulus Plautius from Gaul to Kent, and soon after the Britons had been defeated on the Medway, he joined Aulus Plautius with reinforcements, including a number of elephants. This large army marched into Essex, probably camping at Moulsham before the final advance on Camulodunum, where Claudius received the submission of seven chiefs. Then he returned to Rome after a visit of only 16 days, leaving his troops quartered in the Colchester area.

The conquest of the rest of southern Britain took nearly another 80 years, but, from the beginning, Essex remained firmly under Roman rule, except at the time of Boudicca's revolt. Immediately to the east of Camulodunum a colony known as *Colonia Claudia Victricensis* was set up for retired Roman soldiers where modern Colchester stands. These veterans and the Roman tax-collector treated the native

Coin of Cunobelin

population harshly, so when Boudicca, Queen of the *Iceni,* led the great revolt of A.D. 61, the Essex *Trinovantes* readily joined her. The unfortified *Colonia* was stormed, its Temple of Claudius and other buildings were overthrown and its inhabitants were massacred; then Boudicca and her army moved on to destroy London, St. Albans and all smaller Roman settlements in south-east Britain. In all, 70,000 people were slain before Suetonius Paulinus, the military governor, was able to defeat the Britons and crush the rising.

After peace was restored, the *Colonia* was rebuilt and later enclosed by a massive wall nearly nine feet thick and over 3,000 yards long. Parts of it are still standing; the finest stretch is on the west side where there are remains of the great Balkerne Gate. This spanned the main street leading to the Forum, a large rectangular meeting-place enclosed by colonnades and shops with the Temple in its centre. The vaults of the temple can still be seen under the Norman castle. In the castle itself, now the Colchester and Essex Museum, are many of the thousands of Roman remains found in and around Colchester. These give a clear and full picture of town life in Roman Essex. There are, for example, simple things like a baby's feeding bottle, a child's toy, a lady's mirror, with the brooch and bracelets she wore and the little lamp she carried. There are also rarer objects like the famous Colchester vase of black Caistor ware, with figures of fighting gladiators, and the stone effigy of the centurion Marcus, in full uniform, carved on the tombstone set up by his two freedmen.

There are many remains of the Roman occupation throughout the rest of Essex, especially in the corn-growing lands of the northern half, where Roman buildings have been discovered in 15 parishes. At Ashdon, on the Cambridgeshire border, are the Bartlow Hills—seven Romano-British burial mounds, the finest in Britain; clearly the tombs of rich and important persons. The largest is 40ft. high, with a diameter of 145ft. When it was opened, the burial chamber was found in the centre at ground level. It contained the cremated remains of the occupant in a large square glass bottle, and among the objects his mourners thought he would need in the other world were a bronze folding-chair, a richly-enamelled vessel, a bronze pitcher, bottles and phials of ointment and two bronze strigils for removing moisture from the limbs after a bath. There are fewer remains in the southern half of Essex, then a land of dense woodlands and wide marshes. The deneholes at Little Thurrock and Orsett are considered by many to belong to the Romano-British period. These vertical shafts strike down 50 to 100ft. into the chalk and then branch off into very large chambers. At one time they were thought to be places of refuge or storage pits for corn; but most experts are now agreed that they were chalk workings.

Gladiator Vase, Colchester

16

ROMAN ARCHES in the Bastion at the West end of the WALLS of COLCHESTER, vulgarly called the BALCON, and KING COEL's CASTLE.

1. Ruins of the Balkerne Gate in the Roman walls of Colchester

The Bartlow Hills, Ashdon, all Romano-British tombs of chieftains and other important persons

3. St. Peter's-on-the-Wall, Bradwell, was built by St. Cedd about 654 on the inner wall of the Roman fortress of Othona

4. Greensted Church is unique: its nave of cleft logs is the only known timber building surviving from Saxon England

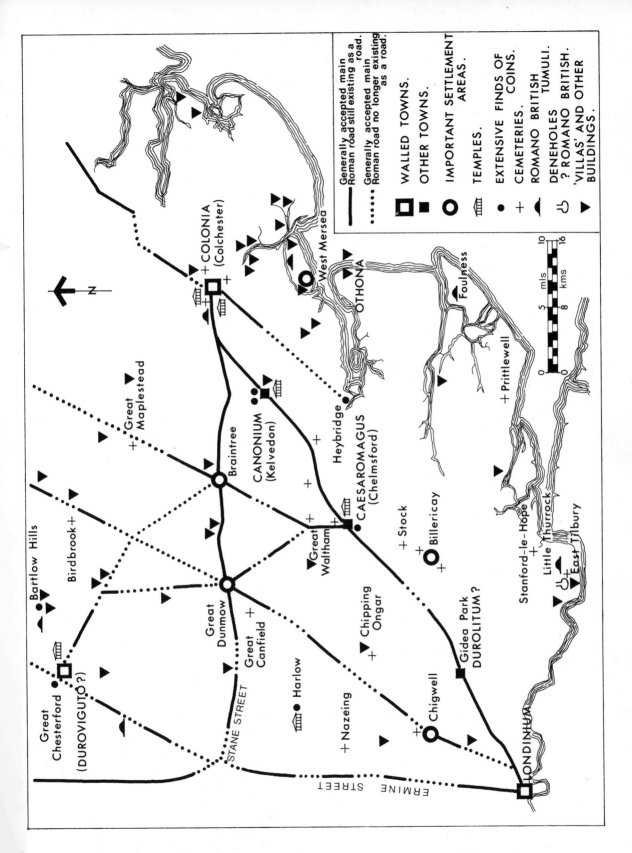

Legend

Generally accepted main Roman road still existing as a road.

Generally accepted main Roman road no longer existing as a road.

- WALLED TOWNS.
- OTHER TOWNS.
- IMPORTANT SETTLEMENT AREAS.
- TEMPLES.
- EXTENSIVE FINDS OF COINS.
- CEMETERIES.
- ROMANO BRITISH TUMULI.
- DENEHOLES ? ROMANO BRITISH.
- 'VILLAS' AND OTHER BUILDINGS.

COLONIA (Colchester)

West Mersea

OTHONA

Foulness

Great Maplestead

Great Chesterford (DUROVIGUTO?)

Bartlow Hills

Birdbrook

CANONIUM (Kelvedon)

Heybridge

CAESAROMAGUS (Chelmsford)

Braintree

Great Waltham

Stock

Billericay

Prittlewell

Stanford-le-Hope

Little Thurrock

East Tilbury

Great Dunmow

Great Canfield

STANE STREET

Chipping Ongar

Gidea Park DUROLITUM?

Harlow

Nazeing

Chigwell

LONDINIUM

ERMINE STREET

N

0 5 10 mls
0 8 16 kms

17

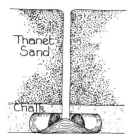

Denehole at Grays

Wherever the Romans extended their Empire they built roads. Their earliest roads in a new province were military roads, made for the rapid movement of troops and equipment; these in time came to be the chief routes for trade and were often linked by a network of secondary roads. This is true even for a heavily wooded area like Roman Essex; but much more has to be found out before a definitive Roman road map of the county can be drawn. The most detailed is in Volume III of the *Victoria County History*; the map shown here gives only those roads accepted by all archaeologists.

Three main roads ran through Essex. The road from *Londinium* to the *Colonia* crossed the county from south-west to north-east and then continued to the Wash. Between London and Colchester there were known to be three intermediate stations—*Durolitum*, *Caesaromagus* and *Canonium*. The exact position of *Durolitum* is not certain; possibly it is at Gidea Park and now covered by buildings. *Canonium* was possibly at Kelvedon; an alternative site is Rivenhall, where the present parish church is almost surrounded by a Roman settlement covering 33 acres. Recent excavations have proved that *Caesaromagus* was more than just a military station. It was built in the angle formed by the present Moulsham Street and Baddow Road, Chelmsford, on slightly rising ground near the junction of the Can and the Chelmer. It was occupied throughout the Roman period and was important right from the beginning, for the excavators found remains of large public buildings which were destroyed, possibly during Boudicca's revolt, and then rebuilt soon afterwards. Even its name *Caesaromagus*—'Caesar's Plain'—is unusual, for it is the only place-name in Roman Britain to have an imperial prefix.

The second main road, often thought to be older than Roman, is Stane Street, running east to west from Colchester to the west Essex boundary and beyond to join Ermine Street, the third great road. One branch of Ermine Street crosses the north-west corner of the county, and in this stretch was the interesting site of a walled town on the east bank of the Cam, just to the north-east of the present village of Great Chesterford. Like so many ancient settlements, it was built on a well-drained river terrace of gravel. In 1948, the gravel was needed for building houses, so there was only just time for archaeologists to explore part of the site before mechanical excavators removed it.

It is now quite certain that the strong well-built walls enclosed a town which was very different from the *Colonia* at Colchester. The soldiers who retired to the *Colonia* were 'Romans' from all parts of the Empire, and they and their descendants were completely Roman in outlook and in the way they lived. Great Chesterford was Romano-

18

British—its inhabitants were Romanised Britons. Probably they adopted Roman dress and Roman ways and were able to speak Latin; but in fact, and, possibly at heart, they were still 'natives' whose ancestors were living in the district long before the Romans arrived. Within their town walls were only two masonry buildings, one probably a large civic centre, and the other a tax office. The remaining houses were all timber-framed with wattle-and-daub filling between the timbers. They were rectangular in plan, the roofs were thatched and the floors were made of gravel and beaten earth—all very different from the substantial buildings of Colchester with tessellated floors and a hypocaust, or central heating system, running underneath them.

In the third and fourth centuries, the Germanic tribes, who were later to conquer and occupy Britain after the withdrawal of the Roman Legions, began to launch their attacks across the North Sea. To defend the coast against the invaders the Romans built a whole system of fortifications extending from the Wash to Portchester. Remains of these forts of the 'Saxon Shore' have been found at Hadleigh and also at Bradwell on the tip of the Dengie peninsula at the mouth of the Blackwater.

The sea has destroyed most of *Othona*, the fort at Bradwell, but at one point the construction of the walling, 12ft. thick, can be plainly seen. On the landward wall stands the Saxon chapel built by St. Cedd. Saltings now cover most of the site, and there, at low tide, pieces of Roman brick, worn smooth by the tides of 15 centuries, may still be found.

FURTHER READING

Rosalind Dunnett, *The Trinovantes.*
C. F. C. Hawkes and M. R. Hull, *Camulodunum.*
Victoria County History, Vol. III.
Warwick Rodwell, *Roman Essex.* An admirable survey, free from archaeologists' jargon.

II The Kingdom of the East Saxons

Saxon brooch, found at Dovercourt

The East Saxons gave their name to Essex but left little evidence behind of the way they invaded and settled in it. Nearly all Anglo-Saxon written records belong to a later date and make few references to early events in Essex. On the whole, archaeology is not helpful; probably most Saxon remains are hidden under present towns and villages. Saxon burials have been found at Colchester, Feering, Broomfield, and Prittlewell, but most experts agree that they belong to a period long after the settlement. An exception is Mucking, where recent excavations have revealed an important settlement, with cemeteries, dating from the early fifth century to the seventh century.

The evidence of place-names is more enlightening. The distribution and number of *inga* place-names and other early or fairly early Saxon forms suggest that the invaders entered Essex by the river estuaries and did not filter in from other areas. The group of settlements from Margaretting to *Ginge Puelle* (now Fouchers) in East Horndon, all bearing the *geginga* (later *ginges*) form, were probably all of one folk or tribe—'the dwellers in the *ge* or district'. The inhabitants of the Roothings were one folk, and so probably were those in the Havering area. The whole of the Dengie peninsula as far inland as Danbury was probably occupied by one tribe, the *Daenningaes,* 'or dwellers in the forest'. Other place-names, such as Thundersley and Widdington, are evidence of the pagan worship of Thunor and Woden.

When, about A.D. 600, the mists clear a little and reveal England divided into kingdoms, the history of Essex still remains obscure. The names and descent of the East Saxon kings are known, but very little besides. They were never more than locally important and generally recognised the kings of Mercia as their overlords. The boundaries of the kingdom roughly corresponded to the modern county, with London, Middlesex (down to the mid-eighth century) and part of Hertfordshire.

When St. Augustine came from Rome in 597 with the first Christian mission to pagan England, he soon converted King Ethelbert of Kent and his people. He sent his companion, Mellitus, to spread the Gospel to the East Saxons, but they drove him out and remained pagan, until, in 653, St. Cedd, a monk of Lindisfarne in Northumbria, came as missionary bishop to Essex. He founded a monastery at Tilbury, but he himself lived at Bradwell-juxta-Mare, where he built the church of

20

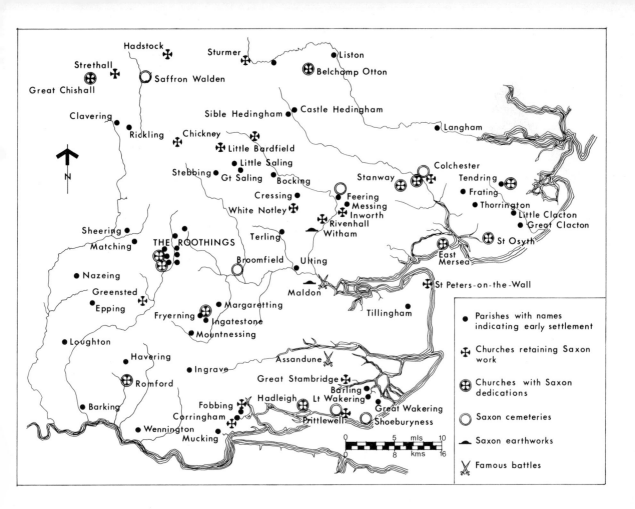

St. Peter's-on-the-Wall on the inner wall of the ruined fortress of Othona. Bede, a monk of Jarrow and the first famous English historian, describes how Cedd's missionary work spread and gathered 'much Church, great Church, to the Lord'. Cedd's church still stands on the Roman wall and is the oldest surviving Essex church by two centuries. The third bishop of the East Saxons was the founder of Barking Abbey, St. Erkenwald, who was consecrated in 675 and took up his residence in London; from that time to 1846, Essex remained part of the diocese of London.

St. Peter's-on-the-Wall was the first of many churches to be built in Saxon Essex. The exact number will never be known. Many were probably made of wood; some of these were destroyed by accident or in war; some were completely replaced by more substantial buildings in later times. The dedication of some churches indicates a Saxon foundation: St. Osyth; St. Runwald, Colchester; St. Albright, Stanway; St. Botolph, at Beauchamp Roothing, Colchester and Hadleigh; St.

21

Edmund, at Abbess Roothing, East Mersea, Ingatestone and Tendring; St. Ethelbert, at Belchamp Otten; St. Edward, at Romford; St. Swithin, at Great Chishall. Some of the Essex estates held by St. Paul's Cathedral and other great English churches may have had churches built on them in Saxon times. Certainly this is true of St. Mary's church, Maldon, probably founded by Ingelric, first dean of St. Martin-le-Grand, in London, 10 years before the Conquest. Over 30 priests are mentioned but few churches are actually named in Domesday Book. Finally, at least 14 Essex churches still have Saxon work in their fabric. Greensted is unique—its wooden nave is the only timber building surviving from Saxon England; it was built about 850. Apart from Greensted and St. Peter's-on-the-Wall, the other Saxon churches in Essex belong to the century before the Norman Conquest.

Christianity in Saxon Essex often suffered from pagan invaders from the sea. One Saxon church dedication recalls a legend of Princess Osyth, abbess of a nunnery at Chich (St. Osyth) in the seventh century, who was martyred by sea-raiders who landed near the village. She refused to worship their gods. Her head was struck off, and immediately a stream of clear water gushed from the spot where she fell. Later, she arose and, carrying her head, walked to the church where her remains ultimately rested. The raiders were said to be Danes, but the early date makes this most unlikely.

The invasion of the Danes or Northmen probably had little permanent effect on Essex. Even place-names of Danish origin, like Thorpe-le-Soken, are relatively few, and the archaeological evidence is extremely meagre. The invaders apparently used the Essex estuaries with their islands, but only as bases for rapid and ruthless thrusts at richer targets than Essex could provide. By Alfred's Treaty of Wedmore with the Danish leader, Guthrum, in 878, Essex with all other lands to the east of Watling Street became part of the Danelagh. Later Danish invasions brought Alfred's armies to Essex. In 886, he occupied and garrisoned London and extended his frontier to the River Lea. In 894 his army destroyed the camp and ships of the Danish chief, Hasten, at Benfleet. In the following year, Hasten's Danes, from their temporary base at Mersea, towed their remaining ships up the Thames and Lea and camped 20 miles above London; but Alfred dislodged them by building forts and obstructing the course of the Lea.

When Alfred's son, Edward the Elder, began to reconquer the Danelagh, he came with his army to Essex in 913 and camped at Maldon, while his great fort at Witham was being constructed to discourage any movement westward of the Danish army based on Colchester. In 920, he was again at Maldon, and in the following year his army stormed and took Colchester. As a reprisal, the Danes besieged

Saxon doorway, Hadstock

22

Maldon, but the garrison held out until relieved and then it counter-attacked. Then Edward came to Colchester and repaired its defences; and from that time Essex remained under his rule.

Danish invasions began again in force during the reign of Ethelred II, when a strong fleet under Olaf Tryggvason sailed up the Blackwater in 991, seized Northey Island and threatened Maldon. The story of the Battle of Maldon is known in some detail from the fragment of a contemporary poem. Brihtnoth, the alderman of Essex, drew up his army on the south bank opposite the causeway leading to Northey. When the tide receded, the Northmen attempted to cross but were cut down by Brihtnoth's men. Then Brihtnoth allowed the enemy to cross unmolested, and in the fierce fight which followed, he was slain and his army was defeated; and the Northmen were bought off by a payment of £22,000.

The last battle with the Danes was fought in 1016. When King Canute's army ravaged Essex on its way towards Mercia, it was overtaken by Edmund Ironside, son of Ethelred, at Assandune. Edmund was defeated, but, later, Canute and he agreed to divide England between them. The site of the battle has been disputed; some historians think it was fought at Ashingdon; others favour Ashdon in north-west Essex, with Hadstock church near by as the minster which Canute built to commemorate his victory. Edmund died in November 1016, and all England came under Danish rule for the next 26 years. By this time, Essex had long lost its standing as a separate kingdom, but the memory of it never disappeared entirely. When Tudor heralds drew up coats of arms for kingdoms or persons who existed before heraldry had developed, they gave Essex the red shield with the three Saxon swords or seaxes on it.

In the last years before the Norman Conquest, the most powerful family in England was that of Earl Godwine of Wessex and his sons. They rose to prominence under Canute, and, when the old Saxon line was restored with the accession of Edward the Confessor in 1042, they led the English party against the court party of Norman advisers. Godwine's son, Harold, was Earl of Essex for six years, and it was he who rebuilt and re-endowed the Abbey of Waltham Holy Cross which Tovi, Canute's standard-bearer, had founded. The church was dedicated in the presence of Edward the Confessor in 1060. Six years later, when Harold, then the last Saxon king, was slain at the Battle of Hastings, his body was brought to Waltham and buried in the church which he had raised.

Holy Trinity tower, Colchester

23

FURTHER READING

P. H. Reaney, *The Place-Names of Essex*.

W. Pollitt, 'The Archaeology of the Rochford Hundred and south-east Essex', Vol. III, Trans. Southend Antiquarian and Historical Society.

Saxon bronze disc,
found at Saffron Walden

III The Middle Ages: The Church in Essex

In the Middle Ages, the Christian Church in England was part of the Catholic Church of which the Pope was recognised as head throughout western Europe. In Essex, as elsewhere, the authority of the Pope was felt. Early in Richard I's reign, for instance, Pope Clement III instructed the Bishop of London, the Dean of St. Paul's and the Archdeacon of London to settle a dispute between Barking Abbey and the Knights of St. John over the ownership of some tithes at Ingatestone. The deed of settlement bears the seals of the three ecclesiastics and states that they were 'delegated by Clement the supreme pontiff'. Even in the later Middle Ages, when the power of the Pope was weakened, most people thought and acted as if Christendom were still firmly united.

In the two centuries following the Norman Conquest, more and more churches, each with its surrounding parish, were founded in Essex; by 1291, most of the parishes had a church and a priest. The parish church became the most important local building. It was often more soundly and solidly constructed than other local buildings, including the manor house. It was carefully planned and furnished for its main purpose; everything was done to lead the minds of men towards the worship of God.

Round tower, Bardfield Saling

It might well be thought that all parish churches throughout the country ought to look very much alike. After all, people everywhere worshipped in practically the same way throughout the Middle Ages. In fact, however, no two churches are alike, and there is more variety among Essex churches than in most other counties. This is a problem which has interested historians and many other people. There is no simple answer. If the local population increased, the church would be enlarged; otherwise it might remain practically unaltered right through the ages, like the Norman church at Hadleigh. If the parish were small, isolated, and poor, like Aythorpe Roothing, there would not be the money available for alterations; if, as at Thaxted in the 15th century, there were wealthy landowners and prosperous townsmen, then the church would be remodelled and made magnificent. Sometimes there was need for alteration when the services became more elaborate; that is why so many Essex parishes enlarged their chancels. Sometimes there was a change in the way people left their money for religious purposes; in the later Middle Ages, many began to give less to the monasteries and more to the parish churches.

25

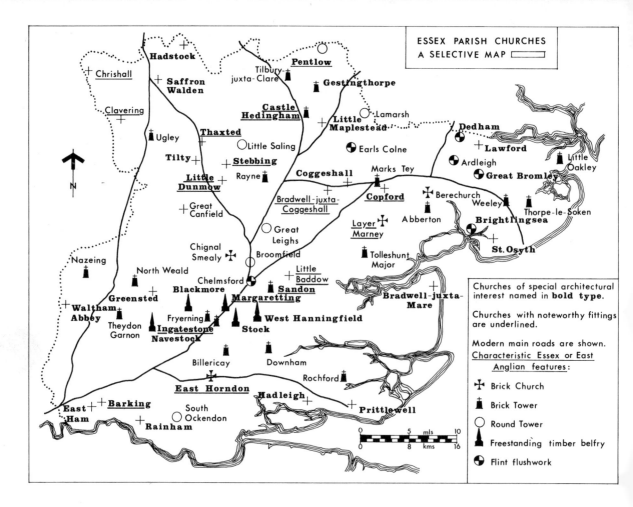

In Essex, there was a special reason for wide variety in the shape and appearance of churches; this was the lack of good building materials, good in the sense of being easily shaped into ashlar. The only stone of this kind in the county was clunch, a hard chalk, but not hard enough to stand up to heavy weathering. Thus, builders were forced to import freestone from the Midlands; its transport was costly, so it was generally used only for essential work, such as arcades, window tracery and quoins. For the rest of the fabric, masons had to make do with 'inferior' local materials—flints, pebble rubble, indurated gravel, septaria and ironstone, as well as bricks from Roman ruins. Even this was insufficient, so craftsmen often used timber and, later, locally-made bricks on a large scale. All this meant that Essex masons and joiners had to use their intelligence and skill to solve problems of construction which did not arise in counties where there was plenty of good building stone. Perhaps the greatest triumphs of the joiners are the remarkable belfries, rather like pagodas, at Blackmore, Stock,

26

Margaretting, Navestock, and West Hanningfield. In the later Middle Ages, masons all over central and eastern Essex built some of the finest church brickwork in England: stately brick towers at Rochford and Ingatestone; handsome brick porches, as at Sandon; brick arcades, as at St. Osyth; and even whole churches of brick at East Horndon and Chignall Smealey. In the northern half of the county, some church walls were faced with flint inlay or *flushwork* in the East Anglian manner.

From the Reformation onwards there have been so many alterations and so much destruction that it is difficult to imagine how the inside of a church looked during the Middle Ages. Fortunately, enough remains for visitors to Essex churches to piece together the story of Christian worship from the Conquest to the time of Henry VIII. The children of Pentlow, for instance, have been baptized at the elaborately carved font ever since Norman times. Then, in the 15th century, the parishioners gave it an equally elaborate wooden cover. The 15th-century Marriage Feast Room stands in the churchyard at Matching. For over 800 years, the communicants at Copford have knelt beneath an apse painted with the figure of Christ surrounded by a rainbow supported by angels. For over 600 years at Little Baddow, the rare and beautifully-fashioned oak effigies of an unknown man and his wife have lain in their carved recesses in the wall. Some of the most interesting churches have been marked on the map on page 26. The double hammer-beam roof at Great Bromley, the stone screen at Stebbing, the stained glass at Margaretting, the wall-carvings at Lawford and Little Dunmow are all among the finest in Essex; but they are only a thousandth part of the heritage which remains.

Essex churches contributed in two special ways to this surviving heritage of English ecclesiastical art: its wall-paintings and its brasses. Of wall-paintings, Sir Nikolaus Pevsner has said that 'any history of the art in England would be incomplete without at least two or three of the works in Essex village churches'; and those who have been privileged to hear Clive Rouse lecturing will appreciate the impact on a largely illiterate medieval congregation of those visual aids, those religious strip cartoons, where every turn of a painted figure's head or hand was charged with meaning. The Copford paintings are the earliest and most important, even though the figures and scenes in the apse were over-restored in the 19th century. The most moving painting is also at Copford: Jairus stands at the door of his house in an attitude of anxious supplication; the head of Christ is turned towards him, His face full of compassion. The most lovely painting in Essex is the mid-13th-century Virgin and Child at Great Canfield; the most dramatic

Blackmore belfry

27

is the late-twelfth-century prophet at Little Easton. An early-sixteenth-century document, headed 'Lyght Kyne', gives a rare glimpse of the interior of a medieval church. It is a list of the sums of money obtained from renting cows belonging to the church to the villagers of Ingatestone. These rents paid for lights in various parts of the church, including those before certain 'images'. These images were all murals; this was proved when during a 19th-century restoration, 'the image of Saynt Christofer', a painting, was discovered in its traditional place on the north wall of the nave, facing the main doorway. Unfortunately it was then re-plastered.

Essex is famous among English counties for its memorial brasses; only Kent and Norfolk can rival its cavalcade of knights, ladies, ecclesiastics, lawyers, merchants, yeomen, and children. Its most noteworthy medieval brasses are at Pebmarsh, Bowers Gifford, Wimbish, Chrishall, Little Horkesley, Latton, and Little Easton. The Little Easton brass shows the decline in design and execution which set in after the middle of the 15th century, but it is still a handsome composition and full of historical interest. It shows the figures of Henry Bourchier, Earl of Essex, died 1483, and Isabella Plantagenet, his wife, died 1485. They lie on a canopied altar tomb moved from Beeleigh Abbey to Little Easton after the Dissolution. The Countess was a Yorkshire princess and aunt to Edward IV and Richard III. She wears a coronet, and her head rests on a tasselled cushion held by kneeling angels. Around her neck is the Yorkist Collar of Suns and Roses. The Earl was a great-grandson of Edward III. He was Lord Treasurer to Edward IV and fought in most of the battles of the Wars of the Roses. He is clad in elaborate 'Yorkist' armour; he wears the Garter, the Garter cloak and badge and the Collar of Suns and Roses, and his feet rest against an eagle, one of the Bourchier badges.

In Essex there are many reminders that a church also had its secular uses as a meeting place and as a storehouse for man's worldly needs. Fragments of armour survive from the days when the safest place for the parish arms was in the church. The strong chests with their three locks originally held the church plate, the churchwardens' account books and the deeds of charities and chantries; later, they came to contain the records of parish government. The 'church ales' were held in the nave of the church; in 1440, Margaret Chyld of Saffron Walden was paid 9d. 'for baking of bread which was at the drinking in the church, and for all the brew'. The church was also the birthplace of English drama. The few early records show that drama flourished in Essex. At Barking Abbey, well before the end of the 14th century, a Sepulchre Play formed part of matins for Easter Day. Later, when religious plays were no longer acted in churches, they were organised

Painting of Christ in majesty, Copford

28

by the parishioners responsible for religious processions and village feasts. Chelmsford and Maldon were well-known centres of dramatic activity, and plays were also produced at Saffron Walden, Dunmow, and Braintree. Neighbouring parishes frequently borrowed from the wardrobe and property-box in the custody of Chelmsford parish church. The contents included a coat of leather for Christ, a Temple and a Hell, as well as a black plate which served as a halo for Judas. One of the plays performed in the Maldon area was 'Master Benet's Christmas Game', written by Benet Burgh, the rector of Sandon.

The parish churches were not the only centres of worship in the Middle Ages. There were also the monasteries—the communities of monks and nuns who had withdrawn from the world to give themselves entirely to a life of religion. In Essex there were 50 religious houses of various kinds, including the great abbeys of Barking and Waltham, the leper hospital at Ilford, the Dominican friary at Chelmsford, and the small alien hospital of the Holy Ghost at Writtle. They are all recorded on the map on p. 51.

Seal of Waltham Abbey

The headship of even the smallest monastery was a position of dignity; in a great abbey it was considerably more. Three queens and two princesses were abbesses of Barking, and all the remaining abbesses down to 1473 came from aristocratic families. The Abbess of Barking was the leading English abbess and ranked as a peer of the realm. She had her own retinue, her own clothing allowance, her own kitchen with its cooks and 'pudding wife'. She had the right to hunt in Hainault Forest and in all woods on the abbey lands. She was not tied down by day-to-day details of convent life. These were the responsibility of the prioress, who was in charge of discipline, and the other senior nuns (sub-prioress, novice-mistress, librarian, chambress, sacrist, fratress, almoner, cellaress), each of whom looked after a department and was assisted by other nuns and by servants. The remainder of the abbey's inhabitants consisted of ordinary nuns who had taken their vows, novices, schoolgirls, young children, priests (since nuns could not officiate at Mass), and a large paid staff, ranging from butler down to menial servants.

The monastic church, where so great a part of daily life was spent by monks and nuns, varied in size and splendour according to the house's wealth and importance; but even in the poorest monastery, as at Latton Priory, it was more imposing than the average parish church. Fortunately, parts of nine monastic churches have survived in Essex, and it is possible to trace the plans of several others. The stately nave of Waltham Abbey, the best Norman work in the county, and the naves of Hatfield Broad Oak, Hatfield Peverel and Blackmore, are all now parish churches. Little Dunmow church is the former

29

The Devil,
Steeple Bumpstead

Lady Chapel of the priory; the ruined nave and fine west front of St. Botolph's, Colchester, are still standing. The fabric of a monastic church, its internal fittings, furnishings and treasures, its clock and bells, were in the charge of the sacrist and his officials. The sacrist of Colne Priory in 1426 kept his accounts with great exactness, even to the penny 'to a certain washerwoman for washing there the towels of the said sacristy'. It was an important duty of the sub-sacrist to sound the bells for mass and the various offices from Matins to Compline. These varied from order to order and from day to day, but were rarely fewer than eight. On some days at Barking Abbey, where the Calendar of Saints' Days was crowded and the services for important festivals were long and elaborate, there were only brief periods when the sound of worship was not heard.

In dignity and importance, the chapter-house came next to the abbey church itself. Here the formal meetings were held: the election of a new abbot, the enforcement of discipline, the sealing of important documents. In his own chapter-house, Abbot John Fowler of St. Osyth was about to be deposed by the bishop's commissary in 1434, when he made a last-minute plea to be allowed to resign. This was granted, and so he saved his right to a pension. The chapter-house surviving at Beeleigh is a particularly gracious and dignified room.

The chapter-house and most of the conventual buildings were grouped around the covered cloister, in many monasteries the only place for contemplation and study, though larger religious houses had separate libraries. Waltham library contained 125 books; among Barking's manuscripts were Aesop's *Fables,* a Virgil and a Cicero. Some of these and other known Essex monastic manuscripts may have been written and illuminated by the monks and nuns of the houses to which they belonged; certainly, when the monks of Colne Priory needed a new register in 1375, 90 parchment skins were bought for 17s. 9d., as well as four pennyworth of vermilion.

The *dorter*, or dormitory, was usually on an upper floor overlooking the cloister. At Beeleigh, it covered the area occupied on the ground floor by the chapter-house, the warming house and a small parlour. Leading off the dorter was the *rere-dorter* containing the privies and lavatories. The chamberlain was responsible for the necessities of the whole dorter range—mattresses, baths, the fire in the warming-house, the linen, clothing and footwear of the brethren. The dorter was the only place where a monk could store any personal possessions, for although every *regular* had to take the vow of poverty and most orders disallowed private property, there is evidence that some Essex monks and nuns had goods and money of their own, including pocket-money, paid out either by the cellarer or the

30

pittancer. At Barking, the 'thirty-seven ladies of the convent' had 1½d. a week.

The cellarer also provided the food for kitchen and *frater,* buildings usually situated off that side of the cloister opposite the church. The Barking cellaress bought vast quantities of wheat, oats, malt, meat, fish, poultry, eggs, and bacon, mustard by the gallon, peas for Lent, beans for midsummer. She paid the brewers and bakers. She had to provide Tyrian wine for the Abbess and a sugar loaf at Christmas. Unfortunately no monastic kitchen has survived in Essex, and only parts of the frater, or refectory, at Beeleigh, St. Osyth and Prittlewell.

In addition to the buildings around the cloisters, there were the infirmary with its chapel, the cemetery and, within most monastic precincts, the fishponds, since monastic houses were always placed near a river or stream. The guest house was usually just within the precincts. Monastic hospitality was often abused by guests: the canons of Thremhall Priory on Stane street complained about 1350 that they were 'too heavily burdened by the cost of hospitality because we are placed so close to the highway'. Round the whole conventual building ran the precinct wall with its great gatehouse and lesser gates. The gatehouse and a stretch of wall are all that remain of the powerful Abbey of St. John at Colchester; the St. Osyth gatehouse is one of the stateliest surviving in England.

Outside the gate was the gatehouse chapel. Two fine examples survive at Tilty and Coggeshall. Near the precinct wall, too, were granaries and other farm buildings; in 1491, Thoby Priory leased to William Rainold the dairy at the gate of the priory, with cowshed, barns, stables and other buildings.

A monastery's responsibilities, however, did not end at its gates. A community living apart from the world could not exist without the income in kind and money from its endowments. Many religious houses controlled certain parish churches—Walden at one time held as many as nineteen. Sometimes a monastery took a share of the tithes and other income of the church; sometimes, it *appropriated* the living and installed a vicar at a fixed stipend. An even larger part of a monastery's wealth came from lands given by the faithful. As early as 1086, Barking Abbey held over 9,000 acres in Essex, over 2,000 in other counties, and 28 dwelling-houses in London.

The scattered lands of a monastery had to be properly managed and farmed. It is very doubtful if any monks, except perhaps the Cistercians and those in the smaller and poorer houses, actually worked in the fields. This was done by the lay brethren, or, if the lands were leased, by the farmer's labourers. Some Essex monasteries appointed a lay steward to manage their estates, but in the larger houses the

Font case, Littlebury

31

Piscina, Barnston

cellarer was in full control, buying and selling lands, granting leases, supervising the farm work and workers, holding manor courts, and keeping careful accounts. One surviving cellarer's roll of Waltham Abbey, 53ft. long, is taken up entirely with a record of all tenants of land in the manor of Epping from 1461 to 1539.

Although monasteries could not have carried on their daily life without the income which came from endowments, it was this same wealth which helped to bring about their decline. They became land-owning corporations, often too much concerned with worldly affairs. They were drawn into disputes with one another and with laymen. In 1375, for instance, John de Silvis, acting for Pope Gregory XI, ordered the Abbot and monks of Walden Abbey to restore to the vicar of Saffron Walden his vicarage and income which they had seized. The greater religious houses were exclusive: only the daughters of aristocratic families were admitted to Barking Abbey until late in its history, when wealthy merchants' daughters could also become novices. People began to think less of the monasteries, to make fewer gifts of land and money to them, and to be less inclined to allow their children to become monks or nuns. This made it particularly difficult for the smaller monasteries to keep going and secure recruits. When Wolsey dissolved Tiptree Priory in 1525, the only *regulars* there were the prior and one other.

In the latter part of the Middle Ages, people who wished to give to religious causes usually made wills leaving lands and money for the endowment of chantries in parish churches. Here masses were said for the souls of the founders and others named by them. In 1349, Robert Travers of Basildon laid down clear instructions: the rent forming his endowment was to be received from the lands held by his bondsmen, Richard Noblepas and 'all his brood'; even the wax left over from the Paschal candle was to be saved towards the candle for the following year. One of Writtle's chantries was founded by the vicar, William Carpenter, under his will of 1531, which stated that the first chaplain was to be John Oxford, formerly Abbot of Tilty. Carpenter's chantry chapel was built on to the body of the church, but many other chantry chapels were set up in an existing aisle or transept without causing any alterations to the fabric of the church.

FURTHER READING

Victoria County History, Vol. II.
A. C. Edwards, *Essex Churches 600-1800*.
A. C. Edwards, *Essex Monasteries*.
J. R. Smith, *Medieval Essex Churches*.

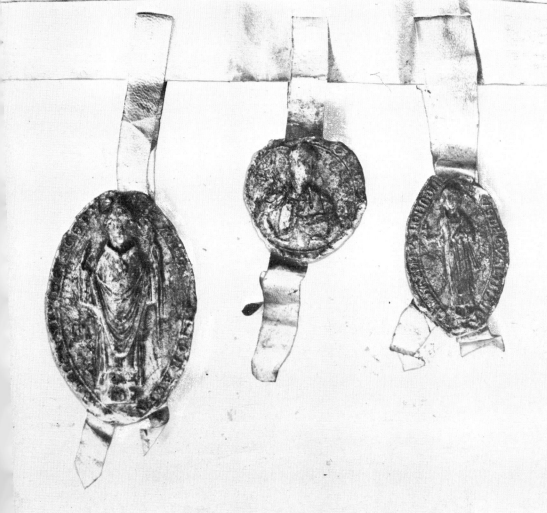

5. Deed of *c.*1195 settling a dispute between the nuns of Barking Abbey and the knights of St. John of Jerusalem about tithes in Fryerning and Ingatestone

6. Brass at Little Easton to the Earl of Essex, Lord Treasurer, d. 1483, and his wife Isabella Plantagenet, aunt of Edward IV and Richard III

Sir Nikolaus Pevsner, *Essex,* in *The Buildings of England* series.
Norman Scarfe, *Essex.* Shell Guide.
E. A. Loftus and H. F. Chettle, *A History of Barking Abbey.*
C. A. Hewett, *Church Carpentry.*

Tiger and Mirror benchend,
Wendens Ambo

IV The Middle Ages: The Land and the People

Bishop Odo, from the Bayeux Tapestry

In the winter of 1085, nearly 20 years after the Battle of Hastings, William the Conqueror ordered a survey of England to be made. In the following year, he sent officials into the counties to find out and record the owner, extent, population and taxable value of every estate and how it was farmed. Most of this information was then written in Latin in two volumes of *Domesday Book*. The smaller volume, the *Little Domesday*, contains the survey of Norfolk, Suffolk and Essex; the larger volume covers the rest of England, except the extreme north. Much of the information is difficult to understand, and some of the places are difficult to identify. Nevertheless, as the historian, Freeman, has written, 'Domesday Book stands alone; no other land can show such a picture of a nation at one of the great turning points in its history'.

It shows that William had turned out most of the Saxon landholders of Essex at the Conquest. Some of the lands he had kept for himself; the remainder he gave in return for military and other services to the army of land-hungry adventurers who had come over with him. The most grasping of these was William's half-brother, Odo, Bishop of Bayeux, who received vast Essex estates, mainly in the south-east. The greatest lay baron in Essex was Eustace of Boulogne. Geoffrey de Mandeville held a compact block of 12,000 acres around his castle of Pleshey and other lands near at hand in Terling, Broomfield, the Leighs, the Chignalls, Mashbury, the Roothings, and Barnston.

Domesday mentions 440 separate places of settlement in Essex, and there was probably a total population of about 70,000. There were only two boroughs: Colchester, with a population of well over 2,000, and Maldon, a royal borough with 180 houses in its urban portion and a population of over one thousand one hundred. The other settlements were fairly evenly distributed over the county, though these were fewer in the south-west, where the forest land was probably thickest. Nevertheless, the higher lands to the north and west of the Roman road from London to Colchester were the more densely populated parts, with the greatest number of plough-teams and meadows; and this area continued to be the most populous part of Essex until London began to spread deeply into the county in the 19th century. This may be partly because the boulder clay of the north was more fertile and less difficult to work than London clay, and partly because the coastal

34

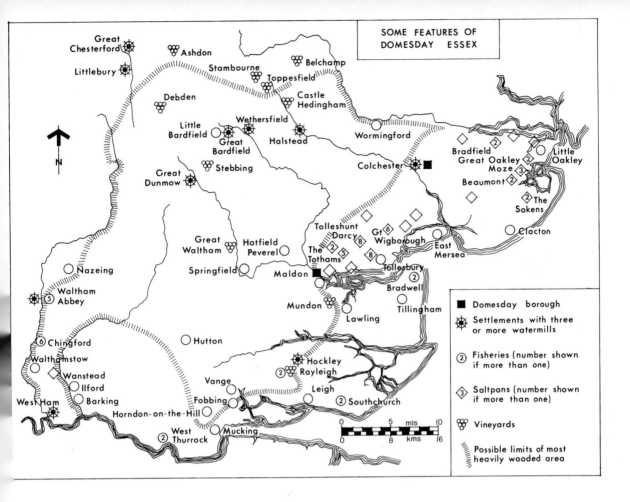

Legend:

- ■ Domesday borough
- ✳ Settlements with three or more watermills
- ② Fisheries (number shown if more than one)
- ◇ Saltpans (number shown if more than one)
- 🍇 Vineyards
- ⟋⟋⟋⟋ Possible limits of most heavily wooded area

marshlands were extensive and continued for centuries to be unhealthy, ague-ridden areas.

Naturally, most of the 28 recorded places with fisheries lay on the coast, particularly along the north bank of the Thames and around the Blackwater estuary. There was another group along the Lea, including six at Chingford and five at Waltham, and isolated fisheries at Springfield, Wormingford and Bardfield. The coastal marshlands supported a surprisingly large number of sheep: there was pasture for 1,300 sheep at Southminster and 700 at Fobbing. The salt-making industry was concentrated in the coastal area of the extreme north-east and the north side of the Blackwater, though there was an isolated salt-pan at Wanstead in the south-west.

Domesday also records the number of mills, vineyards and beehives. The mills were water-mills on the rivers and streams. There were about 230 in all; Ham, now Newham, was specially well-off with eight mills. The vineyards were generally near the castles of the great landholders:

35

St. George and the Dragon, Great Waltham court roll

at Rayleigh, where Swain had his castle; at Hedingham, where the de Vere castle was soon to be built; at Great Waltham, near Geoffrey de Mandeville's stronghold of Pleshey. Bees were important in Saxon and medieval homes: honey was used for sweetening and for making mead, while the wax provided candles for church and home. There were as many as 30 hives at Saffron Walden.

It is difficult to estimate the extent of forest land in 1086, for woodland in any one place is merely recorded for the number of swine it could support. Certainly the Brentwood area, the uplands between the Blackwater and the Colne, and the western part of the county, except the extreme north-west, were heavily wooded. Medieval kings usually regarded most of Essex as Royal forest, but, in practice, the forest area steadily became smaller, and before the end of the Middle Ages it was mainly restricted to the area in the south-west known as Waltham Forest. This is probably why so much of the county was not affected by the enclosing movements of Tudor and Stuart times—it had already been enclosed from forest far back in the Middle Ages, or even earlier.

A number of Essex estates in *Domesday* are actually referred to as 'manors', a word which was used in time for lands held by a lord from the king or another lord in return for services, and cultivated by an unfree population. The word itself came in with the Normans, but the origin of the manor goes back to early Saxon times. After the Norman Conquest there was greater uniformity in the way manors were run, so that later historians were able to talk about a *manorial system*; but, even so, no two manors were ever exactly alike in size and type of agriculture, and every manor evolved its own customs. This is seen in the details of the large number of manor court rolls and other manorial records which have survived in Essex, the earliest known beginning in the 13th century.

One of these, a survey of 1393, gives a detailed picture of life in the large manor of Thaxted. The three open, arable fields were enormous—the holdings on them which formed part of the lord's *demesne* amounted to over 1,050 acres. The rest of the demesne consisted of 113 acres of meadow land, mainly along the Chelmer, 80 acres of pasture, and extensive parks and woodlands, including the 'Great Park' of 672 acres. There were two windmills, the North mill and the Church mill. On part of the manor, the township of Thaxted had already grown up around its magnificent church, which was then being remodelled. In fact, the manor house was in the town itself, quite near the church. Apart from the freemen of Thaxted, there were several classes of unfree tenants: the *molmen* who were liable for labour service on the demesne, but were not usually required to

36

perform it; the villeins or *virgaters,* with 30 acres, and the *half-virgaters* with 15 acres; the *akermen,* who held between 10 and 20 acres; the *coterelli,* with 6 or 7 acres, and the *cotmen,*with only one acre. The *coterelli* and the *cotmen* were probably the descendants of the serfs. Most of the unfree men were eligible to be elected as *reeve* or as *hayward,* and all of them and the freemen, too, were obliged to appear in the manor courts.

In some ways, Thaxted in 1393 seemed to be a 'classical' manor, still running on centuries-old lines; yet there were also many signs of the changes which were bringing about the break-up of the manorial system all over the country. The ancient services, for instance, are all listed in the survey: the week-work, the seasonal ploughing and carting on the lord's land; the *boon-works* or services which the lord could demand at any time; the work required at harvest time. But all these services by 1393 were commuted or exchanged for money payments. Earlier, certain free and unfree men paid rents in kind (poultry, eggs, ploughshares), but these, too, seem to have been commuted. The growth of the township had led to a spirit of freedom. The urban part of the manor was already called a 'borough' and was largely independent of the remainder. The cutlery industry had developed, and there were as many as 30 shops of various kinds in the town. The tenants as a whole were engaged in a sharp dispute with the steward over the customs of the manor, while some townsmen were refusing to pay rent. The lord's arable lands on the open fields were no longer worked by unfree labourers, but were leased out to tenants who were free to cultivate them in any way they wished. Moreover, if any lands reverted to the lord through lack of heirs or any other good reason, the lord did not re-grant them to others on the old basis, but leased them out for a money rent.

The disputes and changes at Thaxted, and a reference in its survey to 'the time of the Rebellion', the Peasants' Revolt, are reminders of the wide unrest throughout England in the second half of the 14th century. The court rolls of Great Canfield, Birdbrook and Blackmore all refer to the Black Death of 1349 which carried away one-third of the country's population. There were no longer enough labourers on most manors to carry on the farming in the old ways. Some lords, as at Thaxted, leased out their demesne lands. Others hoped that the various statutes of labourers against higher wages and prices would be effective. In Essex, the statutes were even more severely enforced than elsewhere; at the Chelmsford Assizes in 1351, 12 men were presented from the Hundred of Chelmsford alone, including Alan Banstrat of Great Baddow, who 'will not serve unless he takes for his salary as much as two others take'. Essex labourers, still bound to

Guildhall, Thaxted

37

John Ball

perform services for their lords, resented these restrictions, while free labourers resented the attempt to keep their wages down.

The smouldering unrest flared into open rebellion over the unpopular poll-tax imposed by the government to raise money for the war against France. Villagers everywhere evaded the tax by making false returns. The revolt, which became widespread, began in Essex on 30 May 1381, when villagers from Fobbing, Corringham and Stanford-le-Hope savagely attacked the king's commissioner who came to Brentwood to investigate and revise the tax returns. The rising spread rapidly and rioting occurred all over the county, the rebels making sure, wherever possible, as at Wethersfield, Wivenhoe and Moze, that they burnt the court rolls bearing the evidence of their villeinage. At Coggeshall, they plundered the manor-house of the sheriff; at Cressing Temple, they burnt the dwelling of Sir Robert Hales; at Colchester, they murdered several Flemings; at Waltham every document in the Abbey was burned. Then there was a general movement towards London, where they joined Wat Tyler and the Kent rebels, who had released John Ball, the Colchester priest, from the Archbishop's prison at Maidstone. Shortly afterwards in his famous sermon at Blackheath, John Ball used a text which became the motto of the downtrodden through the ages—

> 'When Adam dalf and Eve span,
> Who was then a gentilman?'

On 13 June the rebel army entered the city. The events of the next three days have often been described—the continuous pillage and slaughter, including the sacking of the Temple and the murder of Archbishop Sudbury, the meetings between the boy king, Richard II, and the rebels at Mile End and Smithfield, the death of Tyler, and the king's courage and presence of mind. Afterwards, most of the Essex rebels returned home bearing the king's charters, promising the end of servitude and of the restrictions on buying and selling. But, once the crisis was over, it soon became clear that the king's promises were worthless. He marched with an army into Essex. To a deputation of the rebels at Waltham he declared, 'Villeins you were and villeins you are; in bondage you shall abide, and that not your old bondage, but one incomparably worse'. He reached Chelmsford on 2 July and issued a proclamation revoking all charters issued at Mile End; but it was not until the suppression of a second rising in the Billericay area, where 500 rebels were slain, and a third rising at Colchester, that the leaders were executed and order restored.

The Peasants' Revolt seems to have had little direct influence on the break-up of the manorial system. In fact, this was part of a much

38

bigger change which was going on all through the later Middle Ages—the increasing use of money in place of services. The Peasants' Revolt was crushed, but villeinage slowly died out simply because it became a more and more old-fashioned and less convenient way of getting land farmed satisfactorily.

The closing century of the Middle Ages was a time of marked change and a good deal of violence. Essex escaped the main baronial clashes of the Wars of the Roses, but occasionally an example of lawlessness emerges from the records. Thomas Rolf (see marginal drawing) was a respected serjeant-at-law. His memorial brass declares that 'Like a flower he shone out among lawyers', but in 1432 he endeavoured to force Thomas Heynes, a prisoner in Hedingham castle, to bear false witness against his master. 'Quit thee now to my lord', said Rolf to Heynes, 'as us seemeth best, or else thou shalt have indignation of my lord and also perpetual prison'.

Through all changes, the manorial court lived on, and in the 16th century its duties increased and its vigour revived for a time. It continued to deal with petty misdeeds and 'nuisances' down to the mid-17th century. It was also responsible for enforcing locally some of the laws passed by the Tudor government. One burden, however, did not fall upon it but on the unpaid officials of the parish. This was the responsibility for looking after local poor people according to the laws passed at the end of Elizabeth I's reign. Indeed, in the 17th century, the parish became the important unit of local government, and the influence of the manor court steadily declined.

Thomas Rolf, Serjeant-at-Law, Gosfield

FURTHER READING

Victoria County History, Vol. I,
H. C. Darby, *The Domesday Geography of Eastern England.*
Sir C. Oman, *The Great Revolt of 1381.*
K. C. Newton, *Thaxted in the 14th Century.*
K. C. Newton, *The Manor of Writtle.*

V Ancient Boroughs, Markets and Fairs

Seal of Dutch Bay Hall, Colchester, 1571

In Saxon and medieval times, most people made their living by farming and dwelt in scattered homesteads or very small villages or hamlets. Others came to live together in rather larger townships, in places which gave them protection from attack and the best opportunity for trade. In time, a township would try to secure the control of its own affairs. If, like Saffron Walden, the town were firmly in the grip of the lord of the manor, it was difficult to gain these rights; otherwise, especially if it were on royal demesne, like Maldon, it could generally manage to obtain a charter from the king in return for money or services. Among the more important privileges was the right to hold a market on one or more days of the week, and a fair at stated times of the year. With the grant of a fair, as at Halstead, went the right to hold a Court of Pie Powder (*pieds poudreux*—dusty feet) to settle on the spot any disputes which might arise. Recent research has shown that there were as many as 72 townships, some of them quite small, where markets were held in the Middle Ages.

Colchester claims to be the oldest town in Britain; it was already the flourishing capital of south-east Britain when the Roman conquest began (see Chapter I). When Roman civilised life declined and died, the Saxons, who at first were not normally town-dwellers, occupied the town soon afterwards. It was prominent in Edward the Elder's campaigns (Chapter II); and the late Saxon tower of Holy Trinity church and the Saxon dedication of another church to St. Runwald proved that it was continuing to grow. By Norman times it was important. This is clear from the evidence of *Domesday* and from its surviving buildings: the massive royal castle, St. Botolph's Priory and St. Martin's church. Eudo Dapifer, who probably supervised the building of the castle, also founded St. John's Abbey and gave Colchester its Midsummer Fair. Its burgesses soon began to control the affairs of the town, for their customs and their ancient right to hold a market were confirmed by the king's judges when they visited Colchester in Henry II's reign. Its first charter (1189) gave the burgesses liberty to choose their own bailiffs and judge and to hold their own court for all cases. It also gave them control of fisheries in the tidal part of the Colne and exempted them from many dues throughout England. A later charter of Edward II gave the borough its St. Denis Fair on 20 October. The proclamation of this fair used to be on the

40

7. *Virgin and Child* at Great Canfield, a mid-13th century painting of outstanding quality

8. (*above*) St. Osyth's Abbey has the finest monastic gatehouse in England. It was reconstructed late in the 15th century and refaced with flint inlay or *flushwork* in the East Anglian manner

9. (*right*) Earthworks of Pleshey Castle, Norman stronghold of the de Mandeville family. Excavations in the upper bailey have revealed the foundations of later medieval buildings

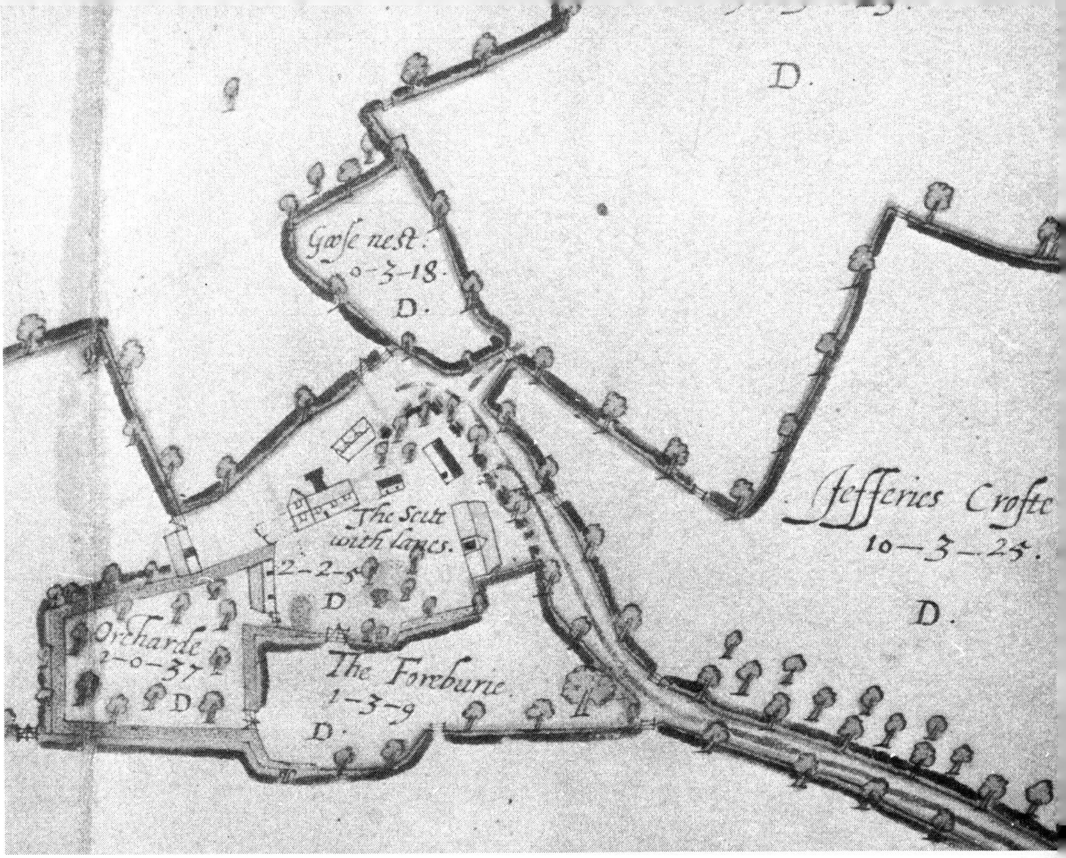
D.
Gose nest.
0-3-18.
D.
The Scite with lanes.
2-2-5
D
Iefferies Crofte
10-3-25.
D.
Orcharde
2-0-37
D
The Foreburie
1-3-9
D.

10. Housham Hall, Matching, a medieval homestead depicted on the map of 1609 by the younger John Walker. Parts of the hall-house and the large 14th century barn still survive

11. Interior of the 14th century barn at Prior's Hall, Widdington

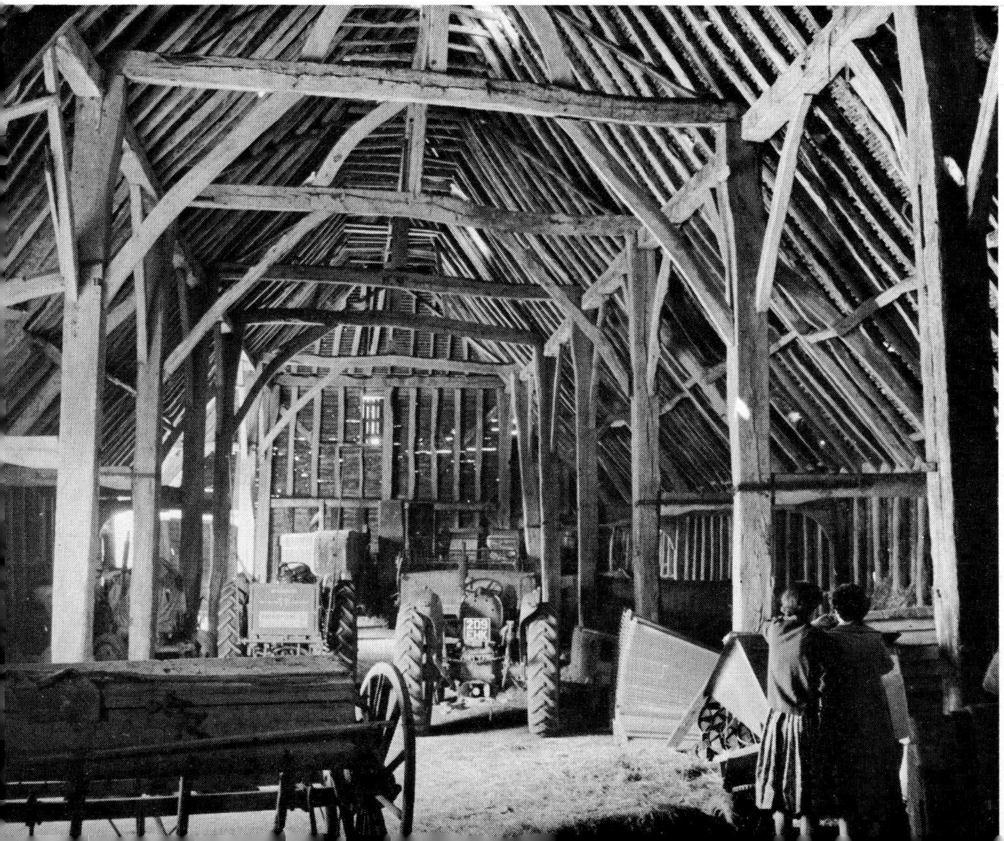

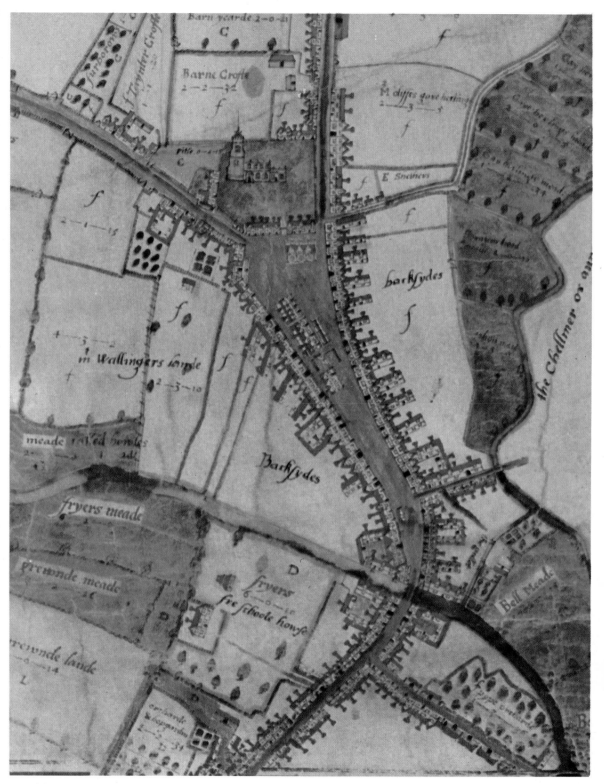

12. Chelmsford, 1591, by the elder John Walker, the first surviving Elizabethan map of a county town

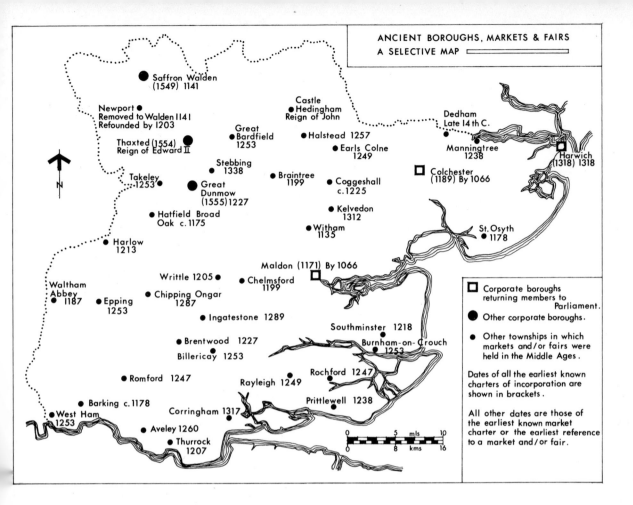

Saffron Walden
(1549) 1141

Newport ●
Removed to Walden 1141
Refounded by 1203

Thaxted (1554) ●
Reign of Edward II

Takeley
1253 ●

Great
Bardfield
1253

Castle
Hedingham
Reign of John

Halstead 1257

Dedham
Late 14th C.

Earls Colne
1249

Manningtree
1238

Harwich
(1318) 1318

Colchester
(1189) By 1066

N

Great
Dunmow
(1555)1227

Stebbing
1338

Braintree
1199

Coggeshall
c.1225

Hatfield Broad
Oak c. 1175

Kelvedon
1312

St. Osyth
1178

Witham
1135

Harlow
1213

Maldon (1171) By 1066

Writtle 1205

Chelmsford
1199

Waltham
Abbey
1187

Chipping Ongar
1287

Epping
1253

Ingatestone 1289

Southminster 1218

Burnham-on-Crouch
1253

Brentwood 1227

Billericay 1253

Romford 1247

Rayleigh 1249

Rochford 1247

Prittlewell 1238

Barking c.1178

West Ham
1253

Corringham 1317

Aveley 1260

Thurrock
1207

□ Corporate boroughs
returning members to
Parliament.

● Other corporate boroughs.

● Other townships in which
markets and/or fairs were
held in the Middle Ages.

Dates of all the earliest known
charters of incorporation are
shown in brackets.

All other dates are those of
the earliest known market
charter or the earliest reference
to a market and/or fair.

0   5   mls   10
0   8   kms   16

day of the civic feast—the Colchester Oyster Feast—still held in October. The Colchester 'natives' are world-famous, and the rents from the oyster fisheries have been a valuable source of revenue to the borough. From the time that Flemish craftsmen came to England in the 14th century, Colchester was the staple town for the cloth industry in north-east Essex. Later, Dutch and Flemish refugees began to weave *bays* and *says,* the new serge-like cloths, in Colchester itself. The industry suffered through the disastrous siege of 1648 (see Chapter VII) and apart from a slight revival in the mid-18th century, it declined steadily and was extinct by the early 19th century.

James Deane's map of 1748 is almost an epitome of Colchester's history. He drew it mainly to record some of the new Georgian buildings he had designed, but, inevitably, the past kept breaking through. The layout of the Roman *Colonia* firmly fixed the shape of the town's subsequent development. The Roman walls are shown with the Balkerne Gate on the west and five bastions on the south-east

41

corner. The Saxon and Norman buildings, mentioned earlier, are clearly marked, with the castle keep already reduced in height and serving as a gargantuan garden ornament in the grounds of Charles Gray, M.P., who lived at Hollytrees hard by. His house and George Wegg's East Hill House almost opposite, with its Gothic summerhouse, are dignified classical buildings indicative of the first half of the 18th century. The old watermills on the Colne and the new windmills to the south emphasise the town's quiet prosperity in the centre of a rich agricultural region, while Deane's little drawings of ships are reminders that so much of its produce was exported from the Hythe to London and the Continent.

In the mid-19th century, Colchester benefited from the coming of the Eastern Counties Railway in 1843 and the branch lines which followed and from the establishment of the Military barracks in 1854–6. Later in Victorian times, industries arrived, beginning with iron foundries. Today it remains a prosperous, vigorous community and, in spite of some modern eyesores, a visually attractive town.

There were prehistoric and Roman settlements in and near Maldon, but the town is essentially Saxon in origin. Its name is Saxon (Maeldune, 'the cross on the hill'), and it was around these crossroads that the main settlement grew up just to the east of the large *burh*. There was a second settlement a little farther down the main road, now the High Street, leading to a third settlement at the Hythe, Maldon's port on the Blackwater. A fourth settlement ran up from the base of a steep hill at the lowest point at which the Chelmer and Blackwater could be bridged. The town's early history is obscure, but it is known that centuries were to pass before those four areas of settlement were to merge. Probably it was beginning to be significant just when it had to face its greatest danger, the Danish invasions of the 10th century. Edward the Elder twice visited the *burh* in his campaigns against the Danes (see Chapter II). Later, in the same century, Brihtnoth fought the battle which has given Maldon a permanent place in national history and literature (Chapter II). By the time of *Domesday* it was an important borough (see Chapter IV), and in 1171 it received its first charter enabling it to hold its own law courts and exempting it from dues elsewhere in return for the provision of one ship when the king went to war. Its customs and privileges, all recorded in its famous *White Book*, grew during the Middle Ages and were jealously guarded, for Maldon burgesses were proud of their independence. Its original charter is lost, but all later charters were kept in Darcy's Tower, a massive 15th-century brick building which became the Moot Hall in Elizabethan times; they are now in the custody of the Essex Record Office. Like most Essex ports. its period

Arms of Maldon

42

of greatest prosperity was probably the 18th century and the first two-thirds of the nineteenth. Just over 100 years ago it had 147 registered vessels, and its fishing fleet numbered thirty. Its exports were corn and oysters; its main imports were coal, oil and timber. When Lord Fitzwalter was rebuilding Moulsham Hall around 1730–40, his timber and other building materials came from Maldon merchants. Like Colchester, Maldon has developed, aided by the Chelmer-Blackwater Navigation and later by the railway. Iron and timber works and allied industries have replaced its ancient cloth and leather crafts. It is still a trading and fishing port and still a meeting-place of main roads and a gateway to the Dengie peninsula. Its Court of Admiralty is dead, but it still looks to the sea, now as a yachting and seaside resort.

Arms of Harwich

Harwich was and still is the county's principal point of exit and entry to and from the Continent. It owes it pre-eminence to its geographical position. It is the only harbour of any consequence between Yarmouth Roads and the Thames. It stands at the mouth of the Stour and facing the mouth of the Orwell, and is built on a narrow north-thrusting tongue of land. It gained its first charter in 1318 and its privileges were increased by later grants, so that eventually it had two markets and two fairs. Like most towns which developed in the later centuries of the Middle Ages, it was laid out on a grid plan, and this street pattern still survives. As a bastion of the east coast defences, it was heavily involved in the Hundred Years' War with France: its walls and gates were erected in 1352; their remains can be seen on the early 18th-century print. To Elizabeth I, as she left it after a pleasant visit, it was 'a pretty town and lacks nothing'. By James I's charter it became a parliamentary borough, sending, like Colchester and Maldon, two members to parliament.

Its shipbuilding industry was probably of great antiquity; certainly it flourished for two centuries after the opening of the Royal Naval Yard in 1657. Not only did men like Sir Anthony Deane and his successors turn out ships for the Navy, but others, like Joseph Graham around 1800, were building vessels for the important packet service, for coastal commerce and for trade with Baltic and other ports. All this and its considerable deep-sea fishery made it a prosperous port from late Stuart times onwards. Defoe said, 'the inhabitants seem warm in their nests, and some of them are very rich'.

Harwich needed this prosperity to mitigate one source of economic instability which has always been a source of pride. This is its long naval tradition which brought wealth and prestige in times of war and neglect when the danger was past. Edward III set out from the port in 1338 on his first expedition against France. It was active in repairing its defences at the time of the Armada, and its sea-captains

Arms of Saffron Walden

gained fame in the naval war which followed. Charles II knew the port well during the Dutch wars, when it was of prime importance in the summers of 1665 and 1666 to his fleets in their desperately fought battles against de Ruyter. Indeed, in every war, including those of this century, Harwich has rendered invaluable service to a nation that depends on its navy to protect its shores and keep open its trade routes.

The coming of the railway and the building of Parkeston Quay in 1883 have contributed to the stability of Harwich, Indeed, its large and efficient ferry service, fed by the railway, is the modern equivalent to the old packet service; Harwich today is *busy*. It is also conscious of its heritage: the care shown by its active amenity society and by private persons for its buildings, those three-dimensional records of its economic history, could well be followed by others.

Saffron Walden has a Saxon name indicating a Celtic origin (Walden, 'the valley of the Wealas', or Britons), and a Saxon cemetery. The medieval town grew up under Geoffrey de Mandeville's Norman castle guarding the main north-west entry into Essex up the Cam valley. His successors as lords of the manor did not allow the town much independence. It did not secure its first royal charter until 1549, and it was not until 1618 that it gained control of the market. How-ever, the market was ancient and important and covered the present centre of the town. Some of the old names have gone, but it is still possible to trace the Butter Market, Tanners' Row, Mercers' Row, Pig Street, and Fish Row, where market stalls were replaced by permanent shops, so that those who merely needed temporary stalls for the weekly market had to move out into the present market place. The wealth which the medieval market brought to the town is shown in the large number of handsome timbered houses and the finest Perpendicular church in the county. Part of the town's prosperity came from the trade in saffron from the purple flower which gave the town its distinctive name and is borne on the borough arms.

Thaxted is described by Camden in 1610 as 'a little market town, seated very pleasantly upon a high, rising hill'. By 1393, as the detailed survey of that year shows (see Chapter IV), it had grown up on part of the large manor of Thaxted. The cutlers had already been there for nearly a century; their industry flourished until the 16th century, and the timbered Guildhall was originally the hall of their craft. When the industry declined, William Bendlowes, Recorder of Thaxted, introduced fustian weavers and clothiers to restore the town's prosperity, but this industry also declined, especially after the Civil War. From 1554 to 1684, Thaxted had its own charter, but, unlike the other ancient chartered towns it was not well enough placed

44

geographically to remain really important. Its greatest era was the 15th century, when rich lords of the manor and prosperous cutlers re-fashioned the famous church and built the fine houses which give so much delight to visitors from richer and less beautiful towns.

The Flitch Chair,
Little Dunmow

Great Dunmow grew up at the point where one of the main north-south routes crosses the ancient Stane Street; other roads also meet there. It was a chartered borough from 1553 to 1885, with a weekly market and two annual fairs. Like other towns in the northern half of Essex, it was a centre for the *bays* and *says* industry. With the village of Little Dunmow near by, it is famous for the Flitch Ceremony. Married couples who apply are 'tried' before a 'court' and are awarded a flitch of bacon if they are proved to have lived in perfect harmony for a year and a day. The ceremony probably originated with an early prior of Little Dunmow and is mentioned by Langland and Chaucer. It died out in 1751, but was revived a century later at Great Dunmow, largely through the influence of William Harrison Ainsworth, the novelist.

Chelmsford owes its early importance to the bishops of London, who held the manor from Saxon times to the Reformation. They built its bridges over the Can and Chelmer, brought it a weekly market and a fair and enabled it by the early 13th century to outstrip its early rival, Writtle, and to become the county town and the seat of the Assizes. At the Reformation, Chelmsford and the neighbouring manor of Moulsham were acquired by the Mildmay family and continued to grow steadily for another four centuries. In 1839, when the railway was being built towards Chelmsford, part of the Mildmay estates was sold. This opened the way for the industrial development of the late 19th and early 20th centuries. It was not until 1888 that Chelmsford gained its charter—nearly seven centuries after it had become the capital of Essex. Since 1914, its medieval church has been the cathedral of the modern diocese of Chelmsford.

A remarkable picture of Chelmsford in 1591 is provided by John Walker's detailed, accurate and visually attractive map, supplemented by the written survey which goes with it. It shows a town approaching the middle of that vast rebuilding period, *c.* 1565–*c.* 1640, but still partly medieval. To the north, in the fork between Duke Street on the south-west and New Street on the east, is the parish church, now the cathedral, 'a goodly, seemly and large building of stone'. To its south, in front of the buildings flanking the churchyard and standing alone at the head of the High Street, is the Sessions House. Here, under a timber-framed umbrella, the Assizes and Quarter Sessions were held, literally in open court. Beside it and running nearly half way down the street is the market area, with its middle row and market stalls.

The town itself was 'well housed and well built for timber and tile', and contained 'more than three hundred habitations, divers of them seemly for gentlemen'. New Street in 1591 was no longer 'new'. Here and in other parts of the town are medieval hall houses. Much of the main High Street seems to have had an Elizabethan face-life, but three-storeyed houses are rare; in fact, the town had just come to the stage when it was beginning to strain at the seams. It had long sent wings backwards towards the 'backsydes', reached by cartways marked in black on the map: soon, its restricted sites would force the carpenters to build upwards. Some of the back wings were already joined to form courtyards; most of these were the larger of the 'many fair inns'. One of these was the *Lion*, near the bridge over the Can, not the Norman bridge, but its successor, built by Henry Yevele, Edward III's master mason. Beyond the bridge was the hamlet of Moulsham, then almost an alien territory.

Apart from Chelmsford and the chartered boroughs there are nearly 20 towns of considerable age. Rayleigh, for instance, grew up under the shadow of its Norman castle, and Waltham around its famous abbey. Both remained as local centres, changing only very steadily up to the middle of this century. At Witham the original settlement grew up beside the Saxon *burh* in Chipping Hill; then, through the efforts of the Knights Templar, a second settlement, Newland, with a planned layout, was built on the main Chelmsford–Colchester road. Some of the former clothing towns are now merely picturesque villages. Some towns have grown with the outward spread of London. One town, Harlow, has had a large new town grafted on it. Billericay, like Brentwood, is an old market town which was not originally an ecclesiastical parish. It is the urban area of Great Burstead, a parish of great antiquity, with evidence of occupation in the Bronze Age, Iron Age, and Roman times. It is a ribbon development on a main north-south road, near the intersection of an east-west route. By the time of the Norman Conquest it was a rich manor with a population of one hundred and thirty. Until about 10 years ago, its long High Street had not changed fundamentally for over 400 years. Epping's mother church is at Epping Upland, but its later main settlement, a ribbon development, like Billericay's, runs along the main London–Cambridge road. It became well-known for its coaching inns: it was the first stop out of London, and the last before reaching it. When Sir John Barrington and his family set out from Hatfield Broad Oak in May 1660 to be in the capital for the Restoration of Charles II, they stopped at Epping for cakes and ale. On their return in September, the bells of Epping greeted them as they passed through and the ringers were given six shillings.

Arms of Chelmsford

The ports are interesting. Manningtree (with Mistley) is still a small river port and agricultural centre. Its golden age lasted from 1705, when the Stour was made navigable to Sudbury, down to the coming of the railway in 1848. Coal was imported from Newcastle and timber from Norway. Wagons would queue to discharge their corn and other agricultural produce for London; the ships would return with mixed cargoes, including dung from the London stables. By far the best picture of Mistley in its heyday is the plan from Scalé's fine survey of 1778. There was also a fair amount of shipbuilding, including the *Amphion* of 914 tons and 32 guns, launched in 1798 and famous for a short while in 1803, when Nelson made it his flagship instead of the larger, slower *Victory*. The market town of Rochford, less important now as a river port, still retains some of its former charm, in spite of the screech of planes overhead, the roar of traffic rushing past its market square, and some not notably sensitive development.

Barking was a lively river and fishing port which grew up beside the great abbey; indeed, it became the most important fishing port in Essex. The Barking well-smack, invented early in the 18th century, enabled fishermen to bring back their catch alive from the Dogger Bank and even beyond, to be eagerly absorbed by the London market. Even as late as the mid-19th century its importance had scarcely declined: there were 140 fishing smacks of 40–60 tons apiece employing over 900 men and boys. Rapid transport of fish by rail, however, ended all this, and Barking is now a lively industrial borough of Greater London.

'High Light', Harwich

In 1565, the pleasant trading and fishing port of Leigh was 'a very proper town, well-furnished with good mariners where commonly tall ships do ride'. Among the 'good mariners' was the redoubtable Andrew Battel, whose fantastic adventures in Brazil and Africa covered nearly 20 years in late Elizabethan times and provided the first account in English of the zebra and the gorilla. There was the Haddock family, famous in the late 17th century and the early 18th, when it produced two admirals and at least seven captains of the Royal Navy. There was Captain William Brand who commanded the *Revenge* at Trafalgar. He is commemorated in Leigh old church by a tablet placed there by his four sons who all lived to see the centenary of the battle. Today, much of Old Leigh and its cockle sheds has been eroded away, but it remains an attractive place in its modern role as a valued partner in the enterprising holiday resort of Southend-on-Sea.

Brightlingsea was a place of prehistoric and Roman settlement, but its continuous history dates from Saxon times. Facing the river entries to Colchester and Maldon with sheltered anchorage on its own creek, it became an important medieval fishing and trading port and an out-port of the Cinque Ports. It supplied ships and men for Edward III's siege of Calais in 1347, for Drake's attack on Lisbon in 1589, and for the Royal Navy at every crisis. When the cloth trade was flourishing it exported cloth to the Netherlands from the Essex weaving towns and even from the West of England. It shared in the wine trade with Gascony, and was importing coal in early Tudor times. Its former eminence is reflected in its large and fine parish church with its notable series of brasses of the Beriffs, a Brightlingsea merchant family. Its oyster fisheries were once important; it is still famous for its sprats. It had a fair-sized shipbuilding industry; it provided 11 ships for the Navy between 1804 and 1807. Seventy years ago, the great yachts raced there, and it is still a summer resort for those who prefer the active pleasure of sailing to the more passive entertainments of large seaside towns.

Some of the north Essex towns were not permanently affected by the decline in the cloth trade. Coggeshall, with a great 'wool' church and many medieval and Tudor houses, including 'Paycocke's' (see Chapter VIII), has changed little since it was famous for its *whites,* 'exceeding any cloth in the land for rare fineness'. It still retains a steady prosperity and so, too, does Halstead, a former *bays* and *says* town. Braintree, with Bocking, has been fortunate. Its engineering and metal work firms have contributed to its growth and prosperity. Moreover, it did not really lose its textile industry: woollen cloth was succeeded by silk, and this in turn by rayon and other fabrics from man-made fibres. Its most visual link with the past is Bradford Street, Bocking, one of the most remarkable streets in Essex and almost an epitome of the town's economic history. Here are the former homes of cloth merchants from the 15th to the early 19th century, and behind some of the classical facades, archaeologists are finding remains of houses which go back deep into the Middle Ages.

By its steady, outward spread, London has enlarged and then engulfed more and more townships and villages in south-west Essex. One of the latest to be swallowed is Romford, now the Greater London borough of Havering. It began as a medieval settlement on the Roman highway from London to Colchester at the point where it crosses the broad or 'roomy' ford, and it became the capital and centre of the Royal Liberty of Havering. To its north were the royal palace of Havering-at-Bower, to the south was Hornchurch which sent its leather goods to Romford market, established in 1247 and still flourishing. In the present century, the large Victorian houses became offices, and a dormitory area grew up on the outskirts of the town. London has now virtually stretched to Brentwood, which began as a ribbon development on the main road to London and well away from the parent settlement of South Weald. It was a halting place for medieval pilgrims on their way to Becket's shrine at Canterbury. Now it is an attractive residential and dormitory town.

Even some of the very small townships had their moments of importance when their annual fair was held. In 1589, Lady Petre visited the village fair at Ingatestone and instructed a London pewterer to turn 'five score and one pound of old pewter into a new fashion'. A delightful map of Latton, 1616, shows the animals and their drovers and the stalls with their holders at the fair on Mark Hall Common.

FURTHER READING

W. White, *Directory of Essex,* 1863 edition.
Victoria County History, Vols. IV, V, VI.
F. W. Steer, *History of the Dunmow Flitch Ceremony.*
J. R. Smith, *Towns of Essex.*
A. F. J. Brown, *Essex at Work.*
Histories, varying in merit, have been compiled for most of the ancient
        Essex boroughs.

VI The Reformation and its Consequences

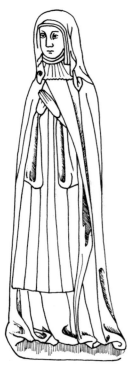

Brass of nun, Dagenham

Almost from their beginning, the religious changes known as the Reformation influenced Essex men and women. This is not surprising, for it was easy for travellers to bring the teachings of Martin Luther and other reformers across the North Sea to Colchester and to spread them among the weaving towns and villages in the north of the county. This alarmed the Church authorities, so, in 1527, they arrested about 40 persons for heresy at Colchester, Braintree and Witham, and, later, another 80 around Steeple Bumpstead. When, however, Henry VIII quarrelled with the Pope and made himself the head of the English Church, his actions, with one exception, probably had little effect at first upon the lives of Essex people. This exception was the Dissolution of the Monasteries.

The religious houses in Essex, as elsewhere, had been declining for many years (see Chapter III). Five of them had long been closed down. Bicknacre Priory died out through poverty in 1507 and, by 1534, Latton Priory was deserted. Cardinal Wolsey had dissolved six other priories and had used their wealth towards the building of his college, now Christ Church at Oxford. Probably the remaining houses were still well conducted, but this did not save them. Henry VIII looked upon them as the last strongholds of the Pope's power and he coveted their wealth in land, which was still considerable. In 1536, he closed down all those with an income of less than £200 a year, and the seven remaining houses had all surrendered to him by 1540. It is almost impossible to state their total yearly income in modern money; perhaps it would be around four million pounds. There were few protests: the monks went quietly; ordinary people showed no sympathy with them, and there were no risings as in the north of England. Only the Abbot of St. John's, Colchester, resisted. 'The King', he said, 'shall never have my house but against my will and against my heart'. He was tried for treason and executed. Most of the heads of the other religious houses were given large pensions; some monks and nuns were provided for, but others seem to have been left to shift for themselves. Occasionally (see Chapter III), a parish bought part of a monastic church for its own use, and occasionally, as at Hatfield Broad Oak, the rest of the monastic buildings became a private residence. Generally, however, the king's agents stripped the monasteries of their contents and roofing and allowed them to fall into ruin. The king then sold the

50

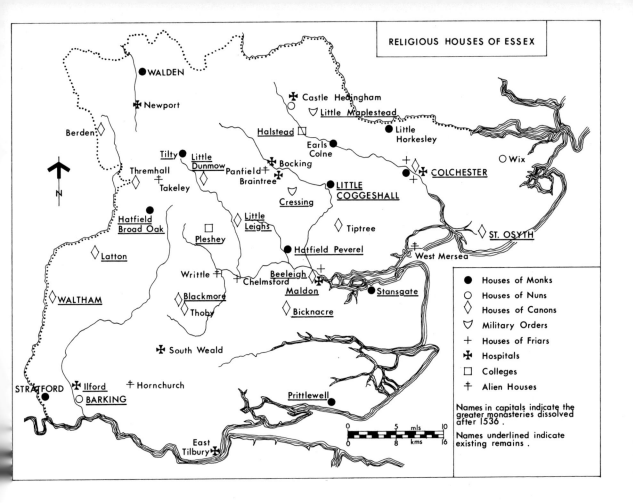

Houses of Monks
Houses of Nuns
Houses of Canons
Military Orders
Houses of Friars
Hospitals
Colleges
Alien Houses

Names in capitals indicate the greater monasteries dissolved after 1536 .

Names underlined indicate existing remains .

monastic estates, totalling about two fifths of the area of the county, to enterprising landowners; it was the biggest changeover in land ownership since the Conquest. Sir Thomas Audley received Walden Abbey and its lands as a gift, but most of the new owners paid the king the full market value—Sir William Petre bought Ingatestone Manor, formerly belonging to Barking Abbey, for £849 12s. 6d., paid by instalments.

A few years later, the chantries and religious guilds, some 50 in Essex, were also dissolved. Their value in money was small compared with the plunder from the monasteries, but their disappearance was a great loss to the religious life and worship of Essex people, and also to education, for nearly every Essex chantry priest had acted as a schoolmaster or as a curate to his parish.

The story of the religious changes in Essex during the reigns of Henry VIII's three children, Edward VI, Mary, and Elizabeth I, is best illustrated in the account books kept by the churchwardens of

Bicknacre Priory

Great Dunmow and other Essex parishes. When, all over the county, the extreme reformers were in power in Edward VI's reign, the Dunmow churchwardens recorded the destruction in their church. The extremists broke up the stone altars and brought in a wooden communion table. They pulled down the rood, with its figure of Christ crucified, from its place above the great screen and destroyed it. They covered the religious paintings on the walls with whitewash, and they bought a new communion book with the service in English, not Latin. When Mary Tudor became queen and the English Church once more accepted the rule of the Pope, the Dunmow churchwardens tried to restore their church to its former state. They bought the old kind of Latin service book and had it richly bound. They brought back the banners for church processions and painted the banner-staves. They paid 'Father Andrews', an old carpenter, for making a cross of timber for a makeshift rood.

Soon the persecution of Essex reformers, or Protestants, began. Some, like Thomas Rose, the vicar of West Ham, fled to the Continent. Others were arrested, tried for heresy, usually before Bishop Bonner of London, and burnt at the stake, either at Smithfield or Islington, or in their own town or village. In all, there were 73 Marian martyrs in Essex. Their courage and cheerful steadfastness strengthened the Protestant cause. When Hugh Lavercock of Barking, old and lame, was tied to the stake at Stratford, he cast away his crutch and comforted his fellow-martyr, a blind man, saying, 'Be of good cheer, my brother, for my Lord of London (Bishop Bonner) is our good physician. He will cure us both shortly; thee of thy blindness and me of my lameness'.

As soon as Mary died, the extreme reformers again attacked the churches. At Great Dunmow, they threw out the altars once more, pulled down the rood-loft, burnt the rood, sold the rich church vestments and set up tablets in the church with the Ten Commandments in English on them. Queen Elizabeth disliked the extreme Protestants and, in 1559, she and her advisers made a moderate settlement of religion, on which the present form of the Church of England is largely based. No choice was allowed: everybody was bound by law to go to church or be fined a shilling. As time went on, it became clear that this settlement was going to satisfy everybody except the staunch Roman Catholics and the extreme Protestants, or Puritans, as they were soon called.

The Puritans wanted what they called a 'purer' form of worship, and they objected to everything which reminded them of the Church of Rome. Their words and deeds often led them into trouble with the archdeacon. The rector of Layer Marney, for instance, disliked

52

wearing the surplice and did not use the ring in marriage or the sign of the Cross in baptism. John Waspe of South Benfleet would not bow at the name of Jesus, and a man and wife at Bobbingworth would not kneel to receive communion; indeed, in some churches the parson placed the altar table-wise in the chancel and provided seats round it for the communicants. Puritans disliked elaborate services and enjoyed long and serious sermons; Robert Winch of North Ockendon, for example, 'refuseth to come to church upon the Sabbath or holy days unless there be a sermon'. For 100 years, most Puritans remained members of the Anglican Church, hoping to reform it from within; but even from the early years of Elizabeth's reign, some Puritans formed congregations of their own and worshipped in secret. In 1586, it was found that John Leeche, the Hornchurch schoolmaster, had a greater congregation in his house than the vicar had in the church. These 'conventicles' were so harshly suppressed that in the early 17th century many Puritans decided to emigrate to America. There were Essex men and women among the first emigrants, the Pilgrim Fathers; the governor of their ship, the *Mayflower,* was Christopher Martin of Billericay.

By Charles I's reign, the Church of England was sharply divided. The Anglican or High Church party, backed by the king, was led by the Archbishop of Canterbury, William Laud, who stood, as he said, for 'order and decency' in the Church. Laud had earlier been rector of West Tilbury. His nephew, Edward Layfield, became Archdeacon of Essex in 1634 and carried out his uncle's policy in his archdeaconry. He ordered Puritan clergy to wear vestments, and at Great Baddow he had the communion table put back at the east end of the chancel and railed in. Opposed to Laud's party were the Puritans, who included the famous preacher, Stephen Marshall, vicar of Finchingfield, and many other Essex clergy. When the Civil War broke out in 1642, most Puritans supported the Parliamentarian side. In Essex, they turned out Thomas Holbeach of Epping and all other Laudian clergy, and conducted their services on Presbyterian lines, rather like those in Scotland. This satisfied most Puritans, but, even so, new sects were formed at Billericay and other places.

Throughout the Commonwealth period the Puritans were in control, but, with the Restoration of Charles II in 1660, the Anglican bishops and other clergy were restored. Parliament then passed laws making it impossible for anyone to be a member of Parliament, a town councillor, or an army officer, unless he took Communion in the Anglican Church and accepted the newly-revised Book of Common Prayer. Most Puritans then realised that their consciences would not allow then to 'conform' to Anglican teaching, so they left the Church and became

Martyrs' memorial, Stratford

53

John Rogers,
Puritan preacher

'Nonconformists'. When, like the 100 persons who met in an orchard at Little Saling, they were caught worshipping in secret, they were often heavily punished. Most of these early nonconformists became known as Congregationalists, but there were other dissenting sects; for instance, the records of the Baptist church at Burnham-on-Crouch go back to 1673.

One group of Puritans, the Society of Friends or Quakers, had always been nonconformists. Their teachings spread among the cloth towns of north Essex, following a visit to Halstead in 1657 by George Fox, the most eminent of early Quakers. They were savagely persecuted by other Puritans during the Commonwealth and by Anglicans after the Restoration; the sufferings of the Colchester Quakers from 1655 have been recorded in detail. Ralph Josselin, the Puritan-minded vicar of Earls Colne, disliked the way they interrupted church services. He wrote in his diary, 'Heard and true, that Turner's daughter was distract in this quaking business; sad are the fits at Coggeshall, like the pow-wowing among the Indies'. In time, however, people became used to the Quakers' plain direct speech and unusual ways, and realised that it was foolish to hate a society which had no ministers, no politics and no desire to use force in their dealings with other men.

Towards the end of the 17th century, the persecution of all nonconformists died down, and in 1689 the law was changed so that most of them could build their own chapels and worship freely. At Little Baddow, for instance, the Puritans used to meet secretly at the farmhouse called 'Cuckoos', and later, more openly at the home of John Oakes, once Puritan vicar of Boreham. In 1708 they built the chapel which is still used as a United Reformed church. By the middle of the 18th century, the laws which prevented nonconformists from holding public offices were repealed or allowed to fall into disuse.

Nonconformity was thus able to flourish in Georgian Essex. Among Congregationalists a congregation was independent—it had its own minister and its own chapel—but it was not inward-looking. In 1798, the Essex Congregational Union was formed, following a meeting at Dunmow, to consider spreading the Gospel by 'preaching it where it is unknown, village preaching by ministers . . . instructing the rising generation, teaching the poor to read by the establishment of schools, or otherwise, distributing religious books and encouraging meetings for prayer, reading the scriptures and religious conversation'. The Baptists relied more on itinerant preachers to spread their teachings; for instance, the Colchester Baptists, who were established at least as early as 1702, were responsible for setting up separate churches at Langham and Earls Colne. At first, Methodism did not flourish in Essex, possibly because the need for it was not as great as elsewhere.

54

The earliest Methodist Church was established at Colchester about 1758, and when Wesley visited the town in 1772, he sadly recorded that 'few of our societies are rich but I know none in the Kingdom so deplorably poor as this'. Among the Quakers there was renewed activity, particularly in the early 19th century, when new meeting-houses were built at Colchester, Chelmsford, Great Bardfield, Epping, and Maldon. Incidentally, a fairly large number of nonconformist chapels have survived. One of the earliest is the former Quaker meeting house of 1674 at Stebbing; one of the most delightful is Potter Street Baptist church at Harlow, built in 1756.

Roman Catholics had to wait much longer before they were allowed to worship in peace and be free and full citizens. When the Settlement of Religion was made, Queen Elizabeth said that she did not wish 'to make windows into men's souls'; but soon it became obvious that England was fighting for existence against Spain, the champion of the Roman Catholic cause. There were also plots against the queen's life and in favour of her heir, Mary Queen of Scots, a Roman Catholic. The laws against Roman Catholics then became very harsh—a priest who said mass was liable to be executed, and a layman proved to be a Roman Catholic could be deprived of two-thirds of his wealth. By the end of the reign, nearly 200 Roman Catholics had been executed, but only one in Essex, the gentle and saintly priest, John Payne, who was hanged at Chelmsford in 1582. Essex Roman Catholics were often brought before the Court of Quarter Sessions or the Archdeacons' courts. Some were members of prominent families: the Petres of Thorndon, the Wrights of Kelvedon Hatch, the Wisemens of Wimbish and Great Waltham, the Paschalls of Great Baddow. Others were humble people like George Binks, the tailor of Finchingfield, who told the magistrates 'that mass is good and confession is good, and that crosses in the church and highways ought to stand to put men in remembrance that Christ died upon the Cross'.

Persecution of Roman Catholics continued in the 17th century, but in the 18th century it gradually decreased. As a result of the efforts of the ninth Lord Petre and some of his friends during the later years of the century, Roman Catholics were allowed to worship freely and establish their own schools and colleges, although they could not hold office or sit in Parliament until the Roman Catholic Emancipation Act was passed in 1829. One interesting result of the growth of toleration in the 18th century was the founding of the first Roman Catholic nunnery in England since the Reformation, when canonesses who left Belgium at the time of the French Revolution settled at New Hall, Boreham, still a Roman Catholic convent and school.

Priest's hiding-hole, Broadoaks, Wimbish

Philip Morant

Meanwhile, as the Stuart Age gave way to the Georgian, the Church of England, the Established Church, continued to hold the allegiance of the majority of Essex people. It lost its urge to persecute and became more rational: there seems to be little evidence of slackness, but the emphasis in worship had changed; a survey of 1763 shows that only in 20 Essex churches was communion celebrated as frequently as once a month; but the sermon remained as important as it had been in Stuart times, although, perhaps, less fiery. Maybe this is epitomised by that remarkable piece of Georgian church-furniture, the three-decker —pulpit, reading desk, and clerk's desk—enabling the services with rare exceptions to be conducted from one spot. As in other ages, so much depended on the individual incumbent, and Essex produced some eminent parsons: Derham of Upmister, scientist and theologian; Strype and Morant, notable historians; Sir Henry Bate-Dudley, sportsman, journalist and busy magistrate. But there is no evidence anywhere of neglect of pastoral care or of anti-clericalism among the laity. Philip Morant was a pluralist and a historian and antiquary, but he was also an active priest at Aldham and a member of the Society for the Promotion of Christian Knowledge. William Cooper of Thaxted spent much of his time visiting the sick and aged; others were active in catechising the young and promoting education.

There is little doubt that in Georgian Essex the consequences of the Reformation had worked themselves out: the Established Church was firmly established and had nothing to fear; the Puritan dissenters had gained nearly all they had striven for, and the Roman Catholics were soon to achieve the same. It was a *quiet* time for religion; the problems to be presented to the churches by industrialisation, by the spread of London into Essex, by agricultural disasters and rural depopulation were all hidden in the future.

FURTHER READING

J. E. Oxley, *The Reformation in Essex.*
Victoria County History, Vol. II, pp. 20-83.
T. W. Davids, *Annals of Nonconformity in Essex.*
Essex Recusant (from 1959: in progress).

VII The Siege of Colchester

Long before the final break between Charles I and Parliament, there were clear indications that most Essex people would be on Parliament's side.The king's action was resented when he restored the ancient boundaries of Waltham Forest so that fines could be levied on all holders of encroachments made since 1301. Some men refused to pay Ship Money; Samuel Sherman and two other Dedham men even refused to collect the tax. There were Puritan disturbances; in Latton church, for instance, four men pulled down and burnt the Laudian communion rails. When Charles attempted to force a prayer book on the Scots, some Essex soldiers refused to march northwards to fight in the Bishops' War which followed.

Sir Charles Lucas

When the first Civil War (1642–46) began, a few Essex gentlemen, including Sir Charles and Sir John Lucas, Lord Maynard and Lord Petre, were strong Royalists, but the county generally was firmly held and administered on Parliament's behalf by a group of Puritan gentlemen, notably Sir Thomas Barrington, working under the powerful Earl of Warwick. Many Essex men fought in the army of the Eastern Association and later, in the New Model Army, ably led by Fairfax and Cromwell.

The New Model Army won the war, but, in 1647, Parliament, jealous of its power, tried to disband it. At that time, Fairfax's own regiment was stationed near Chelmsford and the rest of the army was encamped along the Cambridgeshire border of the county. There were long and stormy discussions in Saffron Walden church, where Fairfax, Cromwell and over 200 other officers met the Parliament's Commissioners; but fortunately for its own sake, Parliament could neither force nor persuade the army to disband itself.

In the following year, the second Civil War began. There were Royalist risings in Kent, Hertfordshire and many other counties, and an invasion of England by the Scottish army under the Duke of Hamilton. Cromwell marched off with part of the New Model Army, first to put down a rising in Wales and then to fight the Scots. Fairfax defeated the Kent Royalists at Maidstone, but most of the beaten troops under Lord Norwich crossed the Thames on 3 June and camped at Stratford. Four days later, they began to march through Essex. At Brentwood and Chelmsford they were joined by Sir Charles Lucas and other Royalists. Some of the Cavaliers came from Hertfordshire;

Sir George Lisle

others had marched from Hyde Park Corner and had cut their way through Parliamentarian troops at Epping.

On 9 June, the leaders of the Royalist army held a council of war at New Hall, Boreham, and decided to march to Colchester. The next day they raided Leighs Priory, the home of the Earl of Warwick, where they seized arms and ammunition; but at Braintree they were less successful: Sir Thomas Honywood and three regiments of Parliamentarian soldiers had already carried off the powder from the magazine. At Braintree, the Royalists turned northwards to avoid Honywood's troops and marched through Halstead and Earls Colne. 'No part of Essex gave them so much opposition as we did', wrote Ralph Josselin, the Puritan vicar of Earls Colne, in his diary. 'They plundered us, and me in particular, of all that was portable, except brass, pewter and bedding.' When the leading troops of the Royalist army approached Colchester along the Lexden road on the afternoon of 12 June, they found the townsmen prepared to oppose them; but Sir Charles Lucas, who was a Colchester man, promised that the town would not be plundered, and they were allowed to enter.

Meanwhile, Fairfax and his army had crossed from Gravesend to Tilbury and marched rapidly through Billericay, Brentwood and Coggeshall to join Honywood's troops outside Colchester on 13 June. He summoned the Royalists to surrender, but Lord Norwich scornfully asked the trumpeter 'how his general did, telling him that he heard he was ill of the gout, but he could cure him of all diseases'. Fairfax then attacked the town and a fierce battle followed in the Maldon road. The Royalists lost many men and were forced back through the Head Gate into the town itself, followed by Fairfax's leading troops. Then Sir Charles Lucas closed the Head Gate and fastened the bar with the cane he held in his hand. A number of Royalists were shut out and taken prisoner; the Parliamentarians who had entered the town were all slain. The attack on the walls near the Head Gate continued until midnight; then Fairfax drew off, realising that he would have to take the town by siege. He made his headquarters at Lexden, sent to Suffolk and London for more troops and began to build a fort between Lexden and Colchester.

It took Fairfax six days to surround and blockade the town, so that the Royalists had time to stock up with food for the siege. Sir Charles Lucas and 1,200 horsemen sallied out into the countryside and came back safely with provisions, sheep and cattle. Another sortie as far as Mersea brought back cattle and five waggons of corn. Two ships from Kent managed to reach Colchester with corn and other provisions before Fairfax blockaded the river at Mersea.

58

Fairfax decided to build more forts and draw a 'Line of Circumvallation' around the town. His engineers completed most of the line by 3 July and brought up heavy cannon from the Tower of London, but the Royalists made daring night attacks and held up work on the forts. The contemporary birds-eye view, reproduced here, shows the siege works as they were towards the end of July, though by that time, Fairfax's outposts were right up against the southern walls of the town. Inside Colchester, food was steadily becoming scarcer and the powder in the magazines was beginning to run out. Before mid-August the point of famine was reached and the townspeople were clamouring for surrender. On 21 August, Lord Norwich threw open the gates to allow starving women and children to make their way to the lines, but Fairfax's guards turned them back. One woman with five small children told the besiegers that 'could they but get dogs and cats to eat it were happy for them, but all the dogs and cats and most of the horses were near eaten already'.

On the same day, the Royalists heard of Cromwell's victory over the Scots. They knew their cause was hopeless, and on 27 August they surrendered. Sir Charles Lucas and Sir George Lisle were taken to be shot outside the castle keep by order of Fairfax. Sir Charles was the first to face the firing squad. After he had prayed, he rose, opened his doublet and called out to them, 'See, I am ready for you; and now, rebels, do your worst'. He fell, and Sir George knelt and kissed his dead friend's face; then, thinking the musketeers were too far away from him, asked them to draw nearer. One of them replied, 'I'll warrant ye, sir, we'll hit you'. Sir George smiled and said, 'I have been nearer you when you missed me'. When he rose from his prayers, he cried, 'I am now ready; traitors do your worst'. He fell immediately as the bullets pierced his body. Lord Norwich and Lord Capel were tried by Parliament. Norwich escaped sentence of death by the casting vote of the Speaker of the Commons, but Capel was executed at the Tower. Fairfax sent some of the Royalist officers to the galleys and transported many other prisoners to the West Indies, but he allowed most of the married private soldiers to go back to their homes. He ordered the unfortunate townsmen to choose between a fine of £12,000 or suffering the town to be plundered by his soldiers. They paid up promptly; then Fairfax handed back £2,000 to be given to the poor, and divided the remainder among the troops.

Arthur, Lord Capel

The siege was a tragedy for the people of Colchester. It ruined their homes and their trade; indeed, the town's cloth industry never fully recovered. It left scars which even now remain to be seen: the ruins of St. Botolph's Priory, battered down by Fairfax's cannon, and the Siege House near East Bridge, still riddled with the bullets fired by the defenders as the besiegers advanced towards the town walls.

FURTHER READING

A. Kingston, *East Anglia and The Great Civil War.*
E. Hockliffe (ed.), *The Diary of the Rev. Ralph Josselin.*
D. T-D. Clarke, *The Siege of Colchester*
G. H. Warlow, 'The march of the Cavaliers from Bow to Colchester', *Essex Review,* Vol. XVII.

VIII The Homes of Essex

In Saxon and Norman times, when the total wealth of Essex was not great and was mainly concentrated in the hands of a few, it is probable that most people lived in small and uncomfortable timber huts which disappeared long ago. Even the 19 Essex castles of the Norman barons, the men at the top, have nearly all gone, leaving only massive earthworks, as at Rayleigh and Pleshey, Chipping Ongar, and Canfield. Most of them were of the 'motte and bailey' kind—a timber or stone keep, on a mound surrounded by a moat, with outer moated earthworks, surmounted by a wall or palisade, enclosing a yard or bailey. Some of them, notably Rayleigh and Pleshey, have been closely examined and assessed in recent years; others deserve serious archaeological investigation, especially Ongar, with its text-book set of earthworks, and Clavering, a pre-Conquest castle of unusual form, built by one of Edward the Confessor's Norman followers. At three places in the county, the Norman keeps have survived. The Saffron Walden keep is small and ruinous. Colchester keep was the largest in England and was well over twice its present height; even now it is most impressive. The best preserved Norman keep in Western Europe stands out for miles around above the little town of Castle Hedingham (see Frontispiece). It was the home for 600 years of the family of de Vere, Earls of Oxford, friends and counsellors of English kings.

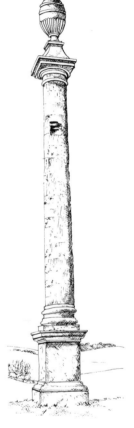

Obelisk at Audley End

Later in the Middle Ages, Essex barons improved their Norman castles. Defence was still important: they retained the keep as a final refuge in time of siege, but they built more comfortable living quarters in the bailey. In Castle Hedingham bailey, archaeologists have traced the foundations of a Great Hall built in the time of Henry VII. At Pleshey, the earthworks have long outlasted all the extensive later buildings except the bridge between the motte and the inner bailey. These later buildings were intact when Richard II arrived in 1397, arrested his uncle and bitter enemy, the Duke of Gloucester, and had him taken to Calais and murdered. They fell into ruin in the 16th century when the castle passed out of royal possession. Richard II himself owned Hadleigh Castle, which his grandfather, Edward III, had completely rebuilt. It has been a picturesque ruin for over 400 years and has been painted by many artists, including John Constable.

Only the most powerful of Essex barons lived in castles, and, in any case, castles were rarely built in the later Middle Ages. Next in size and

61

importance was the manor house, the home of the lord of the manor. A large manor house of the 14th or 15th century, the chief residence of a wealthy lord who owned other manors or estates elsewhere, was generally fortified. In 1414, for instance, Lewis John, a rich money-lender to the Lancastrian kings, was granted a royal licence to embattle the brick house he was building at West Horndon. Even many smaller manor houses were protected by a moat. Unlike the castles, which had usually been faced with costly imported stone, the manor houses were built of local materials. The oldest one in Essex is at Little Chesterford Here, the north-west wing, itself a complete manor house of *circa* 1190, is built of flint rubble with stone facings. The only other medieval stone house in Essex is Prior's Hall, Widdington. Both are on the upper reaches of the Cam, the route by which the stone dressings probably came from the oolite belt, *via* the medieval complex of waterways at the Wash. From late medieval times onwards, larger manor houses, for example, Faulkbourne Hall, were built of brick; most of the remainder were timber-framed, and so, too, were farmhouses, country cottages and town houses.

Knowledge of timber-framed structures has advanced considerably in the past 20 years; they are no longer being studied solely on stylistic evidence. New scientific methods of dating have been discovered and are being perfected. More attention is being given to documentary evidence and, above all, to a detailed study of types of joints and their evolution and of methods of assembly; and much of this work has been pioneered in Essex. The general principles of building in timber have long been known. Timber was used green; trees were rough-hewn where they were felled and, here, sawpits were dug and the main sawing done. The timbers were then taken to a framing yard where the joinery and framing were carried out. Then, the frames, partly dismantled, were taken to the building site and literally reared into position. The plasterers then filled the spaces between the timbers with 'wattle and daub'. They keyed the 'daub' of clay into a 'wattle' of vertical sticks interlaced with hazel or other pliable twigs; then they added more daub until the spaces were filled; then they finished off the filling with a thin coat of plaster. Sometimes they covered the whole of the exterior, including the timber-framing, with a thicker coat of plaster. Later on, in the 17th century, plasterers made patterns in the 'pargetting', or plaster, while it was still damp. The Crown House at Newport, the former *Sun* inn at Saffron Walden, and a house near Wivenhoe church are all decorated in this way.

Plaster figures, Old Sun Inn, Saffron Walden

Essex has a rich heritage of medieval houses. Over 750 were recorded by 1923. Some of these have since disappeared, but many more have been discovered, hidden under later roofs and behind newer

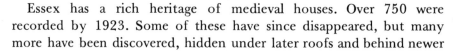

62

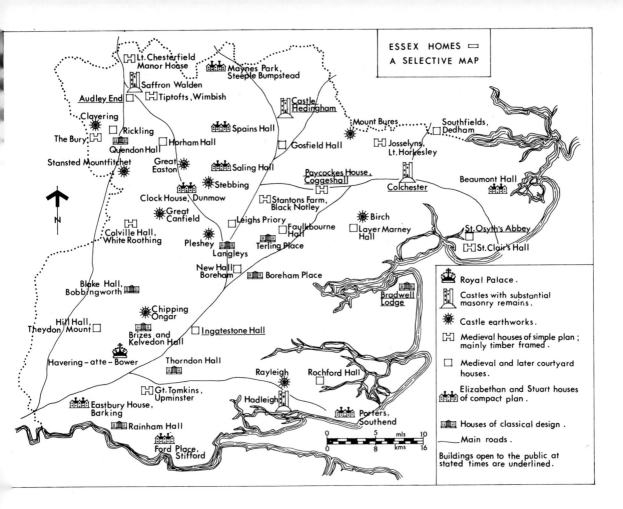

ESSEX HOMES
A SELECTIVE MAP

Lt. Chesterfield Manor House
Maynes Park, Steeple Bumpstead
Saffron Walden
Audley End
Tiptofts, Wimbish
Castle Hedingham
Clavering
Rickling
Spains Hall
Mount Bures
Southfields, Dedham
The Bury
Horham Hall
Gosfield Hall
Josselyns, Lt. Horkesley
Quendon Hall
Stansted Mountfitchet
Great Easton
Saling Hall
Paycockes House, Coggeshall
Beaumont Hall
Stebbing
Colchester
Clock House, Dunmow
Great Canfield
Stantons Farm, Black Notley
Birch
Leighs Priory
Colville Hall, White Roothing
Faulkbourne Hall
St. Osyth's Abbey
Pleshey
Layer Marney Hall
St. Clair's Hall
Langleys
Terling Place
New Hall Boreham
Boreham Place
Blake Hall, Bobbingworth
Bradwell Lodge
Hill Hall, Theydon Mount
Chipping Ongar
Brizes and Kelvedon Hall
Ingatestone Hall
Havering-atte-Bower
Thorndon Hall
Rayleigh
Rochford Hall
Gt. Tomkins, Upminster
Hadleigh
Porters, Southend
Eastbury House, Barking
Rainham Hall
Ford Place, Stifford

Royal Palace.
Castles with substantial masonry remains.
Castle earthworks.
Medieval houses of simple plan; mainly timber framed.
Medieval and later courtyard houses.
Elizabethan and Stuart houses of compact plan.
Houses of classical design.
Main roads.
Buildings open to the public at stated times are underlined.

0   5   mls   10
0   8   kms   16

facades; indeed, some of them are completely incapsulated by later work. Most of these are small or fairly small and all are timber-framed. Some indication of the number of surviving and mainly 'hidden' medieval structures is being provided by the estate maps of John Walker, senior, and his son, John, who were working, mainly in mid-Essex, for 15 years on either side of 1600. These maps have houses and other buildings drawn on them as miniature elevations, and these have been proved beyond doubt to be incredibly accurate. Visits to houses on the site of 'Walker' houses have led to notable discoveries and will eventually supply statistical evidence of the probable number of surviving medieval houses; at present the indications are that there may be upwards of 4,000 of these.

These medieval framed buildings are all *sturdy*; the only existing flimsy timbered houses are some of those built in the 18th and early 19th centuries, when oak was scarce and dear. Very early framed buildings may well have been poor in quality; this is difficult to prove—

the earliest Essex framed structures discovered so far belong to the early 13th century. The *durability* of framed buildings is remarkable: oak has only three main enemies, fire, damp, and the death watch beetle, and if these are guarded against there is no reason why buildings known to be six or seven hundred years old should not last another seven centuries. They are *adaptable* buildings; most of them have been altered again and again to meet changing ways of living. If carefully maintained and not too brutally altered, they are good to look at. At Colchester, Saffron Walden, Thaxted and Coggeshall and in many villages, they blend with Tudor, Stuart and Georgian houses to form attractive streets, which only one other county, Suffolk, can rival. At Coggeshall is Paycocke's House, the home of Thomas Paycocke, a rich clothier. It is of five different medieval 'builds'; the youngest and most famous block faces the street and was built by Thomas Paycocke himself, just before 1500. Southfields at Dedham is another important clothier's home with living quarters, offices and warehouse forming a highly picturesque courtyard. Scattered over country parishes, such as Great Waltham and Felsted, are many more handsome medieval farmhouses. In the past, far too many were neglected and decayed, but in the past 20 years the merits of these buildings are being discovered and appreciated. Some have been professionally restored; more are being reconditioned as a do-it-yourself undertaking by owners who seek and follow the skilled advice which is now readily available.

In a medieval house, whether large or small, in town or countryside, the hall was the principal room and the centre of the daily domestic life of the household. In a manor house it was also the centre of everyday village life, for here the manor courts were often held, and here the orders were issued for the daily farming work on the estate. The name has lasted: there are many 'Halls' throughout Essex, ranging from mansions to small farmhouses.

The hall was lofty and open to the roof timbers, although most halls which survive were later divided into two storeys in Elizabethan and Stuart times. Among the few still open to the roof are Horham Hall, Great Tomkyns at Upminster, and Spurlings and Bridgehouse farms at Felsted. Most of the earlier halls had aisles, like churches. Twenty-six of these remain in Essex. More may well be found; a recent discovery is The Bury at Clavering, an aisled hall of *circa* 1210, disguised in late Elizabethan times. The best known are at Tiptofts, Wimbish, and St. Clere's Hall, St. Osyth; recently, at Stanton's Farm, Black Notley, the accretions of the ages have been swept away and the early 14th-century aisled hall has been restored to its former splendour.

64

3. Maldon from the river, showing St. Peter's tower, the Moot Hall and All Saint's church on the skyline of its hill

4. Thaxted in the early 19th century, with its superb church rising behind its timber-framed Guild Hall

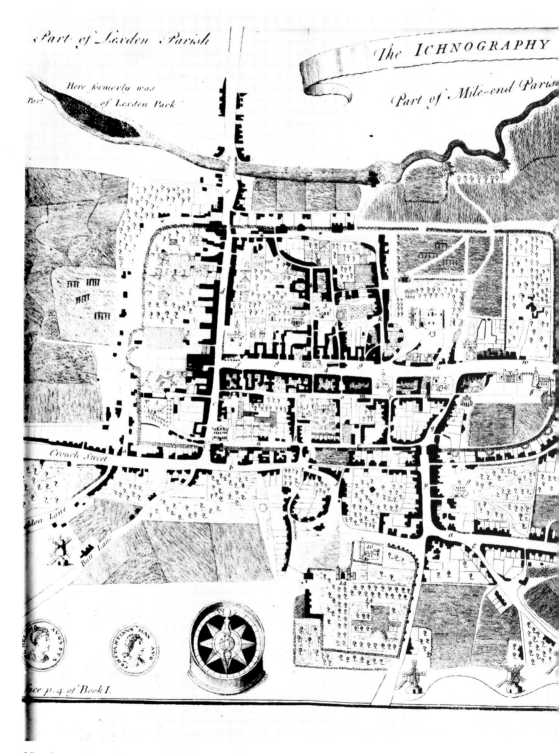

The ICHNOGRAPHY

Part of Lexden Parish

Here formerly was
Part of Lexden Park

Part of Mile-end Parish

Crouch Street

Butt Lane

ice p. 4 of Book I.

15. James Deane's map of Colchester, 1748, shows clearly how the Roman 'colonia' with its walls
has conditioned the later development of the town

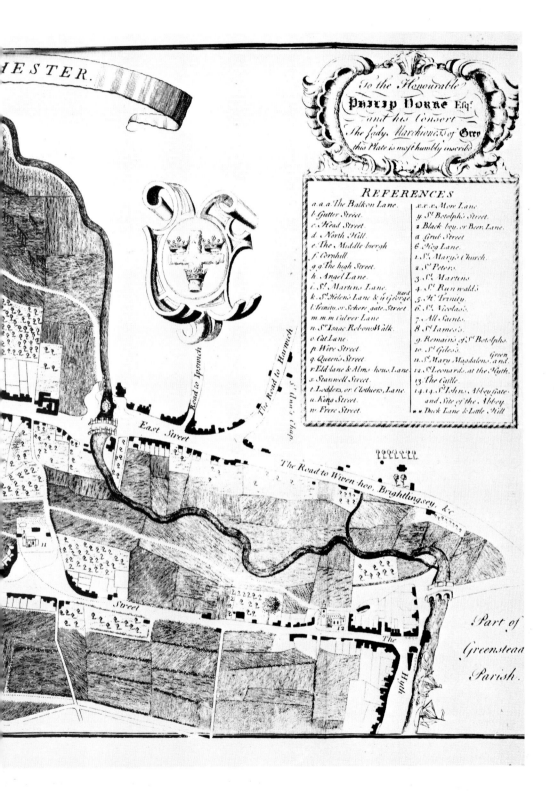

...ESTER.

To the Honourable

Philip Yorke Esq.

and his Consort

The Lady Marchioness of Gr...

this Plate is most humbly inscrib...

REFERENCES

a. a. a The Balkon Lane.	x.x.x Mere Lane
b Gutter Street.	y St. Botolph's Street.
c Head Street.	z Black boy, or Beer Lane.
d North Hill.	a Grub Street
e The Middle bergh	6 Sice Lane.
f Cornhill	1 St. Mary's Church.
g g The high Street.	2 St. Peters.
h Angel Lane	3 St. Martins
i St. Martens Lane.	4 St. Runwald's
k St. Helen's Lane & St. George yard	5 St. Trinity.
l Trinity, or Schere gate Street	6 St. Nicolas's.
m m m Culver Lane	7 All Saints.
n St. Isaac Rebons Walk.	8 St. James's.
o Cat Lane	9 Remains of St. Botolphs.
p Wire Street	10 St. Giles's. Green
q Queen's Street.	11 St. Mary Magdalens. and.
r Eld lane & Alms house Lane	12 St. Leonards at the Hyth.
s Stanwell Street.	13 The Castle.
t Ledders, or Clothiers, Lane.	14.14 St. Johns. Abbey Gate
u King Street.	and Site of the Abbey
w Frere Street.	* * Duck Lane & Litle Hill

Road to Ipswich

The Road to Harwich

St. John's Chapel

East Street

The Road to Wiven-hoo, Brightlingsey, &c.

Street

Part of

Greenstead

Parish.

The

Hyth

A Prospect of the Towne & Harbour of HARWICH
Bullingbrook one of her Maj. Principall Secretaries of State Lord

Humbly Dedicated to the Right Hon.ble Henry Lord Viscount
Lieutennant of y County of Essex & Recorder of y Towne of Harwich

16.   Harwich in the reign of Queen Anne

17.   Barking in the early 19th century, then a busy fishing port on the River Roding

In the Middle Ages and later, across one end of the hall, often on a raised platform, stood the dining table for the lord and his family. His retainers and servants took their meals at tables running down the length of the hall. The benches on which they sat probably served as beds at night, for there were no separate bedrooms, except for the lord and his family. In the middle of the hall, or at one end against a stone reredos, a fire burned in an open hearth, the smoke escaping through a louvre in the roof or through smoke vents in the apexes of the gables, although, even in Norman times, some halls had fireplaces with chimneys. At first the windows were small, without glass, and fitted with sliding wooden shutters; but in the later Middle Ages, a large, glazed bay window was sometimes built on the south side so that the light would fall on the high table. Glazing, however, like most innovations, came in at the top of the social strata and percolated downwards only very slowly; even as late as the end of Elizabeth I's reign, or even later, small houses and cottages still had shuttered windows. The two doorways were facing one another on the sides of the hall, right at the opposite end to the high table, so that the draughts were kept as far as possible from the lord and his family. Across the hall, near these external doors, ran a partition or screen, usually with two doorways in it. On the other side of this entrance passage made by the screen, two more doorways led into the service wing (the pantry and buttery), which was built at right-angles to the hall; the kitchen was usually separated from the house in case of fire, or, at least, semi-detached. At the other end of the hall, behind the high table, was another cross-wing, the 'solar' wing, containing the 'bower' or private rooms of the lord and his family. The 'bower' at Havering-at-Bower, was the country palace to which the kings and queens of England from Edward the Confessor to Charles I retired when they wished to escape for a while from court life. At a much lower social level, however, some hall-houses had only one two-storeyed cross-wing; here the buttery and pantry would occupy the ground floor and above them would be the private room of the lord.

Conduit head,
Little Leighs Priory

It used to be said that the cottages of poorer people had not survived from times earlier than the early 17th century. In the past 12 years or so, medieval cottages have been found, hidden under 17th- and 18th-century alterations, and many more will probably be discovered. One of them was built in the 13th century, but most of them belong to the 50 years on either side of 1500. They are rectangular in plan and are of two, three or four bays in length. If a cottage were four bays long, the two middle bays would be the hall, open to the roof, exactly as in larger houses with hall and cross-wings. The end bays would be ceiled just below tie-beam level to provide two ground floor rooms

Gatehouse, Layer Marney Hall

at either end and sleeping spaces above. Later, usually in the 17th century, the hall was divided horizontally and dormers and a chimney stack were inserted. In Chaucer's *Nun's Priest's Tale*, the poor widow's 'narrow' cottage had only two, or at most, three bays—

'Full sooty was her bower and eke her hall.'

Towards the end of the Middle Ages and in the Tudor period, the standard of living rose and people began to need more space at the solar and service ends of their houses. In a smaller house, as in cottages, they could only obtain this satisfactorily by dividing the hall horizontally and partitioning the new upper storey into rooms; this was done in many old houses still remaining in Essex. In some houses, the hall roof was raised to give taller rooms; in others, the hall was completely rebuilt as a two-storeyed block. In the mansion of a rich man, the additional rooms were spread out around one, two, or even three courtyards. Panfield Hall, Horham Hall, Belhus, at Aveley, Layer Marney Hall, Leighs Priory, New Hall, Boreham, Rochford Hall, Ingatestone Hall, and Gosfield Hall were all originally designed as courtyard houses. Even when new styles became fashionable in Elizabethan and Jacobean times, some great houses, like Hill Hall, Theydon Mount, were built on a courtyard plan. The last and greatest of them was Audley End, completed in 1616. In the 18th century it was reduced to about one-third its original size, but it is still immense.

Like Audley End, part of Ingatestone Hall is now open to the public during the summer months, so that visitors are able to see a handsome courtyard house of Tudor brick. A plan of it is re-drawn here from a map of 1605, showing the house as it was about 50 years after it had been built by Sir William Petre, the Tudor Secretary of State. The entrance then, as now, is at the bottom left-hand corner of the plan. To the left of the drive, the brick granary is still standing. The drive leads to the original gatehouse range, altered a little late in the 17th century. Beyond the gatehouse was the 'base court', flanked on three sides by buildings. Those on the left are still there, practically unchanged, but those on the right have disappeared. An inventory made in 1600 gives the names and contents of all the many rooms around this courtyard. The West Cheese Chamber, for instance, was lined with boards 'to keepe owt rattes'; the fire-irons in the Gatehouse Chamber were almost certainly those bought at Ingatestone Fair on 1 December 1589. Between the base court and the main house was the middle court, enclosed by a brick wall of which only one side remains. To its left was the garden, laid out in trim squares, as was usual in those days. Well to its right was a detached building with two chimneys. This

66

was the Banqueting House, used for picnics, and above it was the School-house Chamber for the Petre children.

The Great Hall range facing the middle court was pulled down about 1800, so that there is now an uninterrupted view from the gatehouse as far as the present front door. The rooms in the south range (on the right) contained 'my Master's Lodging', the kitchens, larders, scullery and pantry. The north range has been considerably altered since 1605. One room, however, the Garden Chamber, looked much as it does today. Then, as now, it had panelling and tapestry work. Its original stone fireplace has a scratched inscription in which the word 'Grey' twice occurs, so it may well be the room where Lady Catherine Grey, sister of Lady Jane Grey, the 'Nine Days' Queen', was imprisoned.

Old Moulsham Hall, from Walker's map, 1591

The finest room in the house is the Long Gallery, running almost the full length of the first floor in the east range. In 1600, it was panelled and was furnished with a large table, a shove ha'penny board and 17 chairs and stools, mostly all richly upholstered. On the panelling hung 'nine painted shields with posies upon them' and seven pictures, including the portrait of Sir William Petre which is still there. The elegant furniture there today belongs to later periods. The walls are lined with portraits of the Petre family through the centuries in ruff and doublet, lace and cravat. Here, from time to time, the music of Elizabethan composers is heard, as it was when William Byrd, the greatest composer of them all, spent Christmastide, 1589, with the Petres, and five musicians of London earned 60 shillings 'for playing upon the violins'.

In Elizabethan times, the courtyard house began to go out of fashion and rich men often built taller and more compact houses. Eastbury House at Barking, was one of the earliest and was followed by Moyns Park, Steeple Bumpstead, Clock House, Dunmow, Spains Hall, Finchingfield, and Porters at Southend. These and later houses, like Ford Place, Stifford, were more conveniently arranged than the court-yard type; but they were still somewhat irregular in appearance, their roof lines were still broken by gables, and the great hall was still the most important room. Quite a number of smaller houses, especially in towns, were built in this more modern compact style, but throughout the first half of the 17th century, the majority of ordinary houses were still planned and constructed in much the same way as smaller houses a century earlier. Apart from a decorated plaster ceiling or a richly-carved fireplace here and there, the Essex homes of Elizabethan and Stuart times were scarcely influenced by the important changes in building which were taking place on the Continent.

*   *   *   *   *   *   *

67

Dovehouse, Writtle Park

In the Middle Ages and long afterwards—as long as agriculture was the dominant industry—a home was a good deal more than a house; existence depended on *outbuildings*. A medieval farmer did not expect much more comfort than a roof over his head and a fire in the winter, but his *barns* were all-important: his wheat barn housed his bread for the year, and his barley barn, his beer and cattle food. The medieval barns of Essex have been disappearing at an alarming rate over the past 50 years, but many remain and are now more carefully guarded. Their carpentry was of the highest standards; their appearance is imposing—they are like the naves of vast rustic cathedrals. The most famous in the county and, perhaps, in the world are those at Cressing Temple. The barley barn is the older; it is now generally agreed that it was built in the 12th century, perhaps within a few years of the manor being granted to the Templars by Stephen's queen. The wheat barn, even larger, was built about 1260. Few of the smaller early farm buildings of Essex have survived: an occasional late medieval granary; some cartsheds which may have medieval elements. The Walkers' estate maps of Elizabethan and early Jacobean times give panoramas of farm complexes which had scarcely changed since the Middle Ages. The younger Walker shows Housham Hall, Matching, in 1609, with two thatched barns, one to the right, the other to the left, both still standing. The larger barn, probably of the 14th century, lost a couple of bays around 1900; the smaller barn is Elizabethan. The other outbuildings, an open thatched cartshed, a small tiled stable and two larger buildings, one thatched, one tiled, have all disappeared. The site is probably older than any of the buildings: the moat around the orchard and 'The Foreburie' suggest antiquity. The thatched farmhouse with an open hall and one two-storeyed cross-wing, is of a type common from the late 14th to the early 16th century. The cross-wing survives, but with a Georgian roof; the hall was completely replaced by a late Georgian building, with some of the original timbers being re-used.

*   *   *   *   *   *   *

For a long time, European architects had followed the teachings of Andrea Palladio (1516–80), who had shown how the styles of ancient Greek and Roman buildings could be used as models. His ideas had some influence on English architects of the age of Sir Christopher Wren, but did not spread widely throughout England until the 18th century. The largest classical or Palladian house still remaining in Essex is Thorndon Hall, designed by James Paine for the ninth Lord Petre, and most of this has been a shell since the fire of 1878. The grandest and most celebrated was Wanstead House, begun about 1715 by Colen Campbell and destroyed in 1823. Audley End, an earlier house, was altered by three of the most famous 18th-century architects, so that it is now as much a Georgian as a Stuart building. About 1718, Sir John Vanbrugh built the magnificent stone screen and staircase at the end of the great hall. Between 1762 and 1770, and again in later years, Robert Adam re-modelled some of the rooms and built a circular Temple in the park and the stone bridge over the Cam, while at the same time the greatest English landscape architect, 'Capability' Brown, laid out the grounds and quarrelled with the owner, Sir John Griffin, over the payment.

Sherman's, Dedham

Meanwhile, all over the country, somewhat smaller country houses were being built: Boreham House, Langley, Blake Hall, Brizes, Terling Place—these are only a few. One of the most delightful, Bradwell Lodge, designed by john Johnson, 1781-86, is joined to a Tudor timber-framed house. In the towns of Essex and many of the villages are small houses of the classical period, with plain regular fronts built to form a straight skyline, tall sash windows and graceful doorways with fanlights. Colchester is specially rich in Georgian town houses. Perhaps Saffron Walden comes next, followed by Harwich, Coggeshall, and Witham. Among the small townships, Dedham is pre-eminent; here the Georgian houses fit in very happily with buildings of earlier centuries.

A large number of so-called Georgian houses, great and small, in the countryside and in town and village street, are like Audley End— really Georgianised. Essex gentlemen unless they were very grand, like Earl Tilney at Wanstead and the ninth Lord Petre at Thorndon, saw no point in pulling down their ancestral homes if these could be altered to give at least lip-service to Georgian fashions; and where the gentry led, the prosperous middle classes were quick to follow. Some were content to put up a classical facade and re-model the front rooms; others carried out more thorough re-modellings. An interesting example is Lawford Hall with its attractive mid-18th-century front and its back wings still much as they were when built in 1583. At Moulsham Hall, Lord Fitzwalter, grand but tight-fisted, arranged matters skilfully. He engaged the Palladian architect, Leoni, to rebuilt his Tudor courtyard house, a side at a time, and he spread the work out over 21 years. In this way he was seldom short of accommodation and he was able to pay the cost out of current annual income. In all these classical houses of the 18th and early 19th centuries, whether great or small, the hall now lost the importance it had in earlier times. In the larger houses it is merely a vestibule around which other rooms are grouped; in the smaller houses it is little more than a passage containing the staircase.

*   *   *   *   *   *   *

Loughton Hall

Medieval houses were inward-looking; a medieval Essex man's home *was* his castle, his refuge, and this way of thinking persisted. The plan of 1605 shows Ingatestone Hall much as it was when built in the 1540s. It is *enclosed*: there are three courtyards, and the main house is ranged around the innermost one, farthest from the entrance drive. The orchard and formal gardens are enclosed by a brick wall with little turrets, some of them 'to kepe in foules', but all are faint echoes of past ages when defence was paramount. It was not until around 1700 that gardens and grounds, while still formal, began to stretch out tentatively towards the surrounding countryside. Then followed the great Georgian age of landscape gardening, when gentlemen employed landscape architects to tame nature skilfully and create carefully-planned settings for their mansions. The most famous of these, Lancelot ('Capability') Brown worked in Essex, notably at Audley End and Thorndon. Humphry Repton, scarcely less famous, worked from his home in Hare Street, Romford: possibly his best surviving Essex layout is at Rivenhall Place. Richard Woods was another Essex landscape artist. In his designs for the grounds of Brizes, Kelvedon Hatch, he included 'A ladies' walk, enriched', a delightful Georgian touch.

*   *   *   *   *   *   *

From the Norman castle right down to the early Victorian villa there was a steady line of development which can be traced clearly in Essex buildings. The line began to be blurred in later Georgian times, when there was a fashion for revivalism in architecture, beginning with Gothick, popularised by Horace Walpole and his friends and followers. By the early 19th century, other bygone styles were being copied. But generally there was some understanding of these past art-forms among eminent architects. Thomas Hopper, for instance, who built Chelmsford Gaol, worked superbly in several styles: Tudor, at Danbury Palace; 'Jacobethan', at Wivenhoe Park; Italianate, at Birch Hall. Then, about the middle of the 19th century, the line broke. Many more styles from the past were being copied and applied in unsuitable ways; sometimes the styles were mixed together. Some Victorian houses were made to look like baronial castles; others were given Gothic windows; others bristled with little turrets like a French chateau. A few architects like Norman Shaw, who designed Chigwell Hall in 1876, and Eden Nesfield, who built Loughton Hall two years later, struggled to make architecture less pretentious. Possibly not enough credit has yet been given to George Sherrin, an architect working mainly in mid-Essex in the closing years of the 19th century. Meanwhile, the spread of London and the partial industrialisation of Essex towns—and the lack of any town planning—led to the building of thousands of miserable sub-standard houses for the lower middle and working classes. In parts of West Ham, for instance, there were open sewers, no paving or lighting, and roads made impassable by deep ruts and pot-holes. In the early years of the 20th century, architecture became even more debased; it was then that imitation timber-framing—'Tea-shoppe Tudor'—became very common. Hundreds of ugly houses are still springing up, but, for the past 50 years there have been more well-designed houses built in Essex than at any period since about 1850. The age of the great house is past, but the age of the New Town has arrived: Harlow and Basildon have been giving enterprising architects an opportunity to plan and build Essex homes which meet people's needs, look pleasant in themselves and fit easily into their surroundings. Harlow has been particularly successful in its civic, ecclesiastical and domestic buildings. Basildon's main contribution, perhaps, has been in industrial architecture.

Belmont Castle, formerly at Grays Thurrock

FURTHER READING

Victoria County History, Vols. IV, V, VI.
Sir Nikolaus Pevsner, *Essex,* in *The Building of England* series.
Norman Scarfe, *Essex.* Shell Guide.
Harry Forrester, *The Timber-framed Houses of Essex.*
C. A. Hewett, *The Development of Carpentry, 1200–1700. An Essex Study.*

Wheat Barn, Cressing Temple

71

IX Old-established Essex Grammar Schools

At a time (1977) when all old Essex grammar schools now maintained by the local education authority are almost certain to disappear, it is fitting that their history should be set down and remembered. The earliest records of Essex schools belong to the Middle Ages when the Church was the guardian of learning. Monasteries and nunneries educated their own novices, but few of them kept schools for other children. Barking Abbey, rich and important, may have been an exception; under its care were schoolgirls and small children, including two little Tudor boys, who became the father and uncle of Henry VII. The oldest Essex schools were usually run by secular priests who served the chantries and religious guilds in townships such as Great Baddow and Coggeshall. When the chantries and guilds were abolished in 1547, some of these schools disappeared. The original grammar schools at Colchester, Chelmsford, Saffron Walden, Braintree, and possibly Coggeshall, survived. Colchester Royal Grammar School, first mentioned in 1206, was re-founded by Henry VIII in 1539; Chelmsford Grammar School, a 14th-century foundation, was re-founded by Edward VI; Chelmsford bears the Tudor royal arms, and so, too, did Saffron Walden Grammar School, re-founded by Edward VI and closed during the present century. Braintree Grammar School seems to have died out in the mid-17th century. In the 15th century there were two grammar schools in Maldon, but there are no links between these and the present school, founded in 1608 by Ralph Breeder, a haberdasher and an alderman of the borough.

Thomas Heron, schoolboy, with ink-horn and pencase

Throughout Tudor and early Stuart times, a fairly large number of people showed their belief in the value and advantages of education by founding new schools. Some founders were probably fired by enthusiasm for the 'new' classical learning of the Renaissance which spread from Italy to other countries. Others were mainly concerned to give poor boys an opportunity to rise in an age when there was a good deal of movement from one social class to another. Some grammar schools, poorly endowed, died out in the course of time; some became primary schools; others struggled along until they were rescued and revived by local education authorities in modern times. The schools of the three most distinguished founders, Sir Anthony Browne, Lord Chief Justice (Brentwood, 1558), Richard, Lord Rich, Lord Chancellor (Felsted, 1564), and Archbishop Harsnett (Chigwell,

72

1629), are still independent schools. Felsted has carefully preserved its Elizabethan schoolhouse with its panels and beams, scored with the initials of boys who worked and played there from 1564 to 1865. In Brentwood Old School building is the incised foundation stone placed there by Sir Anthony Browne's step-daughter, Dorothy, and her husband, Edmund Huddleston. Earls Colne Grammar School was founded about 1519 by a well-to-do clergyman, Christopher Swallow. Walthamstow Grammar School was founded in 1527 by Sir George Monox, a wealthy draper, who had been Lord Mayor of London. Three schools, Dedham, Halstead, and Newport, were founded by women. The story of Newport Grammar School's origin is told by Alexander Nowell, Dean of St. Paul's, who did more than any man to encourage grammar school education in Queen Elizabeth's time. When Mistress Joyce Frankland lost her son in an accident, Dean Nowell tried to console her. 'Comfort yourself, good Mrs. Frankland', he said, 'and I will tell you how you shall have twenty good sons to comfort you in these your sorrows which you take for this one son'.

Sir George Monox

These Tudor and Stuart schools and the re-founded medieval schools were called *grammar* schools because the boys were set to learn the rules of Latin grammar from the moment they began school at the age of seven. At Newport Grammar School a boy had to know his grammar before he was allowed to study the works of Roman authors, and he was not permitted to learn Greek and Hebrew until he was familiar with his Latin texts. Colchester Grammar School boys were encouraged to write and *speak* correct Latin. The Chigwell master was ordered to read to his boys only 'the ancient Greek and Latin poets, no novelties nor conceited modern writers'. All boys were to be brought up in the teachings of the Anglican Church. At Colchester, the boys heard the Lord's Prayer and other prayers, the Confession, the Creed and the Ten Commandments every morning and evening; they went to church twice on Sundays, and were instructed once a week in Dean Nowell's catechism. Boys were expected to be well-mannered. At Saffron Walden they were taught to behave at table—they were not to pick their teeth, or blow their noses without a handkerchief, or drink with their mouths full. Holidays were brief by modern standards: Chigwell boys, for instance, had short breaks at Easter, Whitsuntide, and Christmas, and lessons for Newport boys stopped at three p.m. on Saints' Days. At most schools the day began at six o'clock in the summer and seven o'clock in the winter, and ended at five or six in the evening. During most of this time the boys were expected to get down to their Latin—there were no mathematics, sciences, modern languages, English literature, history or any other modern subject to relieve the monotony of the long day. There were no organised games and little other recreation, though Newport boys were given time for running, throwing darts, and practising archery, and Chigwell boys had an hour off for play on Thursday and Saturday afternoons. It was an exacting life for teacher and taught. The Chigwell master was expected to be 'severe in his government' and 'no puffer of tobacco'. As the Saffron Walden master and boys entered their school every day, they saw the stern motto over the door—*Aut disce, aut doce, aut discede*—'learn, teach or leave'.

FURTHER READING

Victoria County History, Vol. II, pp. 501–564.
H. E. Brooks, *William Palmer and His School.*
M. Craze, *A History of Felsted School.*
J. H. Johnson, 'Chelmsford Grammar School', Vol. LIV, *Essex Review.*
G. H. Martin, *The History of Colchester Royal Grammar School.*
A. D. Merson, *Earls Colne Grammar School.*
W. J. Petchey, *Maldon Grammar School 1608–1958.*
G. Stott, *A History of Chigwell School.*
F. Thompson, *Newport Grammar School, Essex.*
N. Rowley, *Education in Essex, c. 1710–1910.* Seax Series, 8.

X Georgian Essex

In September 1714, a young Essex man, Richard Barret, wrote home to his father, Dacre Barret, at Belhus, Aveley, describing how he had watched the ship bearing the first of the Georges pass by Gravesend and had then gone to Greenwich, where the King landed at dusk by torchlight. Later that night he was presented to the King and the Prince of Wales. He had witnessed the beginning of the Georgian Age.

Agricultural trophies, from Mistley Survey, 1778

Life in Georgian Essex was certainly more civilised than in earlier times. There was a growing spirit of toleration in religion: nonconformists were able to take part in public life, and the most offensive laws against Roman Catholics were abolished (see Chapter VI): From the rich landowners downwards there was, in the earlier part of the period, a greater sense of security than at most times in English and Essex history. It was a good time to live in for those who were not very poor, or sick in mind or body, or very sensitive. There was, however, a grim side. Smallpox marked the thousands it did not kill. Ague, or malaria, still infested the Essex marshes. Men and women ate and drank too much, suffered as a result, took large doses of primitive and useless medicines and died much sooner than they need have done. Medical science and public health improved, but only very slowly. Laws were still harsh. Public executions were still common sights—the map of 1777 shows the gallows lining the north bank of the Thames.

The first 80 years of the Georgian period were a golden age for Essex agriculture, when some of the finest farming in England was practised in this county. The great landowners took a keen interest in their estates, and most of them sensibly granted long leases to their tenant farmers. There were also many independent farmers who possessed their own farms. The size of farms, whether freehold or rented, varied considerably. There were a few very large farms in the coastal areas, but, generally, 400–500 acres were considered a big holding, and the average was probably 150 acres. The small farmers worked very hard, but could do little more than earn a bare living. The larger farmers were enterprising, well-informed and practical. They chose their ploughs carefully to suit the types of land they farmed and experimented to improve them; one landowner, C. C. Western (afterwards Lord Western) of Kelvedon, even tried out the plough-breast invented by Thomas Jefferson, the third President of

75

the United States. They held strong opinions on the best kind of seed wheat for their own land; they worked out their own systems of crop-rotation; they quickly bought the new threshing-machines which were coming on the market. They drained their lands with infinite care, some of them using the mole-plough invented by Thomas Knight, the Thaxted clock-maker. Some made their own contributions to scientific farming. Pattison of Maldon improved the common sowing basket and built special styes for fattening hogs, so that a 70lb. pig would put on another 70lbs. in 28 days.

London easily absorbed all that Essex farms could produce. The capital was growing rapidly, though it did not spread over the Essex borders until late Georgian times. Long before this, however, the London builders pushed out the London market gardeners into East and West Ham, Plaistow, Ilford and Barking. By 1760, Plaistow was famed for its potatoes. The market gardeners of Barking and East Ham soon began to cultivate other crops as well—apples, plums, walnuts, currants, cabbages, turnips and asparagus. They sent their produce to the London market in large, four-horse waggons, fitted with broad-tyred wheels which would not cut up the ill-made roads so badly in wintertime. They kept their land fertile with stable manure from London, brought down the Thames and up the Roding, and unloaded within easy reach of the market gardens. By the end of the Georgian Age, however, London was beginning to cross the border, and the market gardeners were pushed further eastwards to Rainham and other Thames-side villages.

The London market was not the only reason for the agricultural prosperity of Essex. Like Suffolk, it had a long start over many other counties, for so much of its arable and pasture land had been enclosed direct from forest ever since the Middle Ages. Only in the extreme north-west and in a few other places was the land cultivated in the open-field, strip system. In addition, scattered over the county, were several thousands of acres of unenclosed commons, heaths and waste lands, as well as the forests of Epping and Hainault. All this unenclosed land was regarded by larger farmers as an 'intolerable nuisance'. Arthur Young, the greatest of agricultural writers, was a particularly strong advocate of enclosure, though he criticised the way in which enclosures were carried out, especially when they brought hardship to the cottager. In the late 18th and early 19th centuries, much of this under-developed land was steadily enclosed. One of the earliest was the enclosure of Nazeing Common in 1770. This was not an enclosure in the usual sense: the land itself was not parcelled out and the rights of cottagers were maintained. Some of the later enclosures of commons and wastes did bring the bad effects which Young feared: the land was improved

Mr. Dunkin's Pig Case, Maldon

76

in value, but the cottager was no longer able to keep and feed a cow and a few geese.

In Georgian times, Essex was still a county of villages and small towns, all mainly dependent on agriculture, and all running their own affairs with little interference from outside. London was the rich customer but not yet the powerful invader. The map of 1777 shows Leyton, Leytonstone, West Ham, Plaistow, East Ham, Barking and Ilford as villages, hamlets and small townships, all separated from one another. Only along the highway at Stratford, in West Ham parish, had London's vanguard pushed across the frontier. Colchester (population 11,500 in 1801) was easily the largest Essex town. In the later Georgian Age, the South End of Prittlewell was becoming well known as a small seaside resort for the well-to-do, and the quiet little village of Walton-on-the-Naze was beginning to attract a few annual visitors (see Chapter XIV). The other seaside resorts did not exist. There were no railways, and the main roads had only recently been improved (see Chapter XII); so most people rarely went far from their own town or village. Malting, brewing and corn-milling were prosperous industries; one family, the Marriages, have been Essex millers from the late 17th century to the present day. There were also industries which have now died out. Down to 1790 in the Saffron Walden area, the saffron crocus was still cultivated for its stigma or 'chives', which were used in medicine, cooking and dyeing. Hops were being grown on a fairly large scale, especially in north Essex, around Castle Hedingham. Shops in Colchester were still selling sticks of candied eryngo, made from the roots of the sea-holly. The cloth trade was declining, but its place was taken to some extent by the introduction of the silk industry in the Braintree area and in the Lea valley, and by the straw-plaiting industry fostered by the Marquis of Buckingham in the Gosfield district. There were calico-printing works in Waltham and West Ham, and the first and some of the finest English china was made for a short while in the 18th century on the Essex side of Bow Bridge. On the coast of Essex, especially at Brightlingsea and Walton, the wives and children of fishermen gathered nodules of 'copperas' (bisulphide of iron) from the cliffs. These were manufactured into green vitriol (ferrous sulphate) for dyeing clothing and leather and for making black ink. From the quarries of Purfleet and Stifford, waggons, full of chalk and lime for Essex farms, tore up and blocked the roads of south-east Essex.

Life was hard and hours were long for poorer people in the 18th century, but all classes were gay, and often unrestrained in their leisure time. The great families were familiar with the world beyond the county. Lord Fitzwalter lived part of the year at Moulsham Hall,

Bow China figure

Edward Bright's
waistcoat

rebuilding his house in the classical style and adorning it with pictures and statues by the leading painters and sculptors; but his public duties at Westminster and his close contacts with the Royal Family caused him to spend much of his time at his town house in Pall Mall. He also travelled regularly to the spas at Bath and Tunbridge Wells. The somewhat less wealthy attended the local clubs and assembly halls which sprang up in the towns and some of the villages of Essex. They visited the Strawberry Gardens at Sible Hedingham and the theatre at Castle Hedingham. They drank the spa-waters at Witham and bathed in Dr. Tunmer's sea-water baths at Wivenhoe. The prosperous farmer lived pleasantly enough. He could go up to London for the day to buy gold bracelets for his wife and a toothpick case for himself; he could afford a piano, pay nearly £3 to his wife's hairdresser and spend over £100 a year on spirits and port. Rich and poor alike enjoyed country sports and pastimes—the field sports, the racing at Galleywood, the football at Great Tey on Trinity Monday. In an age of heavy drinking and gambling, many of these events were organised by publicans to attract customers. In 1761, Essex played Kent at cricket in the field beside the *Crown* inn, Billericay. In 1787, at the *King's Arms,* Burnham, the gentlemen of the Dengie Hundred fought a main of cocks against the gentlemen of the Rochford Hundred. The patrons of the *King's Arms* at Harwich in 1753 could watch the dancing bears, trained 'to foot it to a violin, both in comic dances and horn pipes, even beyond imagination'. At the *King's Arms,* Colchester, in 1762, Mr. Powell, the London fire-eater, filled his mouth with red-hot charcoal and broiled a slice of mutton on his tongue. Crowds flocked to the rowdy pleasure fairs held all over the county, particularly the famous Fairlop Fair held around the ancient Fairlop Oak in Hainault Forest.

In Georgian Essex, the Justice of the Peace was the most important local personage. With his fellow justices in the Court of Quarter Sessions, he tried all criminal cases except the most serious, and dealt with a great deal of county business, supervising highways, bridges, gaols, houses of correction and county finance, and generally keeping an eye on the administration of the poor law and other government measures. In his own neighbourhood he presided over the petty sessions; his signature and that of a brother justice were often required on parish documents.

The government of each parish was decided in the vestry meeting, presided over by the parson, and was carried out by the parish officers —the churchwardens, the overseers of the poor, the surveyors of the highways, and the constables. The parish was originally an ecclesiastical unit, but, as time went on, its civil duties grew, and particularly its duty, under the various poor laws from Elizabeth I's time onwards, of looking after its own poor inhabitants. The Woodford parish records, for instance, show in great detail how the churchwardens and overseers tried to deal with this difficult and costly problem. They sent back poor 'outsiders' to their own native parish so that they should not be a burden on the Woodford rates. They set up a workhouse for their own poor, they discharged an unsatisfactory workhouse master, and they made an agreement with a Dr. Rice for medical attention to the poor. They settled a bill of £29 8s. with Charrington's brewery for six months' supply of workhouse beer, and they paid rewards to the Bow Street Runners for capturing two vagrants 'having housebreaking implements in their possession'. They apprenticed six children, the youngest aged five, to Morley's silk mills at Waltham Holy Cross. Finally, in 1836, they sent six old men and eight old women from their workhouse to the West Ham Union House because all parishes had then ceased to be individually responsible for their own poor.

Britain was often at war with France during the Georgian Age, but it was the long struggle around the turn of the century which most closely affected the lives of Essex men and women. When Napoleon prepared to invade this country, Essex became an armed camp. The Martello towers at Clacton and other places are reminders of the measures to fortify the coast and the Thames estuary. Millers and bakers were ordered to state how much corn they could grind and how many loaves they could bake in an emergency. Parishes were required to make detailed returns so that the sick, aged, and young persons and the live and 'dead' stock could all be moved inland, leaving a barren Essex for an invading army. Everywhere the militia was called out and volunteer troops were raised and trained. Chelmsford became the northern hub of the defences of London in case Napoleon should try to use the long sea-route and land on the Suffolk and north-east Essex coast. Regular troops were quartered in the district, engineers built defences across the high ground from Galleywood to Moulsham, the streets of the town were congested with waggons and other transport of war. The local 'Home Guard', the Loyal Chelmsford Volunteers, took their duties seriously, but not too rigorously. When they went to camp for a fortnight at Braintree in April 1804, Lieutenant Gepp, a Chelmsford doctor, took sixty-six items of clothing, as well as his chessboard and chessmen, his cards for cribbage, his flute, and a patent toasting fork!

During the war, the poor became poorer. Farm workers' wages rose from six or seven shillings a week in 1750 to about double that amount at the end of the century, but they fell far behind the rise in prices. The declining cloth trade was killed by the war, for Napoleon became master of Europe and cut off England's Continental markets.

Martello tower, Clacton

79

Upminster windmill

Everywhere the parish poor rates rose alarmingly, especially when variations of the 'Speenhamland' system were introduced, by which poor relief was given according to the price of corn and the number in a poor man's family. Parish vestries with consciences tried desperately to grapple with the problem: Woodford, in 1795, started subscription lists for reducing the price of bread for the poor and providing potatoes, firing and flannel.

After the war, Essex shared the nationwide depression. The slump in agriculture affected even the great landowners, though they were cushioned by the extent of their wealth and protected against low corn prices by the new corn laws. For the farm labourers at the other end of the scale it was a time of agonising distress. They were prevented by law from forming trade unions. If, as some did in 1816 and 1829-31, they burnt their master's ricks and barns and smashed his threshing machines, they harmed the source of their own miserable income. These rioters were harshly suppressed: in 1829–31, four were hanged for arson, and at least 23 machine breakers were transported. The Speenhamland method of relief encouraged the lazy labourer and lowered the dignity of the honest worker, though, at least, it saved thousands from the alternatives of starvation or a grim existence in workhouses. Soon this, too, was taken away under the new Poor Law of 1834, which ushered in an even more gaunt and bleak age for those on whose toil depended the maintenance of Essex agriculture, for long to remain the chief industry of the county.

FURTHER READING

Victoria County History, Vol. II, pp. 313–476, *passim.*
Arthur Young, *Agriculture in Essex.*
A. C. Edwards, *English History from Essex Sources, 1550–1750,* pp. 149–173.
A. F. J. Brown, *English History from Essex Sources, 1750–1900.* An invaluable book.
A. F. J. Brown, *Essex at work.*
R. G. E. Wood, *Essex and the French Wars, 1793-1815.* Seax Series, 9.

18. Romford market with old St. Edward's church in the background

19. Dedham is still the most visually-attractive town in Essex. John Constable attended the school on the left of the picture

The Siege of COLCHESTER by the Lord Fairfax as it was with y̆ Line & Outworks, 1648.

Mile end Church.

Col. Fothergall's Fort.

Horse Guard

Road to Hostd

Foot Gd

Col. Envers League

Horse Gᵈ

Horse Gᵈ

Ingolesby Fort.

Col. Ingolesby's Foot Quartrs

The Great Broom Heath

The Town Water House.

Col. Scroop's Horse Quarters.

Col. Envers Quartrs of Foot at first.

Cambridge Road.

Crouched Fryars

Grimsted Howse burnt.

Malden Road.

London Road.

Road to the

Lexden Head Quartrs

Foot Guard

Essex Fort.

train of great Guns

Horse Guard

Barksted Fort.

Col. Cooks Foot Quartr

Col. Pennyruddocks Foot Quarters.

4 Comp of y̆ Lᵈ Waruicks Regimⁿᵗ

5 Comp. of Col. Barksteds Regiment Quartr

Col. Hartackerden's Horse Quarters.

The Generals Quartrs of Horse.

3 Troops of y̆ Lieut. Gen. Horse.

20. Panorama of the Siege of Colchester, 1648

21. St. Clere's Hall, St. Osyth, a timber-framed aisled hall-house of the 14th century

22. The 12th century Barley Barn at Cressing Temple is part of a world-famous farm complex--the Barley Barn itself, the 13th century Wheat Barn, the farmhouse and the early 17th century granary

XI Parliamentary Representation

Before the passing of the great Reform Act of 1832, Essex had been represented in Parliament by its two knights of the shire and by two members from each of the boroughs of Colchester, Maldon and Harwich.

There had been Essex knights of the shire at Westminster since 1290, and from 1430 they had been elected by the votes of the forty-shilling freeholders—those who held freehold land worth 40 shillings or more a year. From the 17th to the 19th centuries, when party feeling ran high, the great landowners sometimes tried to intimidate the smaller freeholders, but generally the elections were freely and vigorously fought. The hustings or platform was set up in Chelmsford, the county town. Here the candidates were nominated amid the cheers and boos of the crowds. Then, from all parts of the county, the freeholders, wearing scarves and cockades (blue for the Tories and orange for the Whigs), would ride over the rough highways and byways into the town to record their votes openly and verbally and to enjoy the unlimited supply of free beer at the Chelmsford inns. Even as late as 1868, the successful candidates, the new knights of the shire, were girded with their sword of office. No wonder the county elections were immensely popular: they provided entertainment which was colourful, rowdy, and entirely free—except to the candidates who footed the bills! Anything might happen—in 1830, an unsuccessful candidate, Squire Conyers of Copt Hall, Epping, barked like a dog from the hustings, 'addressed the electors as "brother calves" and yelled 'Tally-ho!" in the midst of his speech'.

In the 18th and early 19th centuries, Harwich was a Treasury borough, a government 'pocket' borough. Only the mayor and a small group of aldermen and burgesses had a vote. They usually elected government nominees, and in return they were given profitable government posts, such as collector of customs or agent for the government packet-boats.

In Colchester and Maldon, the freemen (i.e., the majority of the burgesses) had the right to vote, though many who lived outside Maldon became freemen of the borough by gift, purchase or inheritance, or by marriage to a freeman's daughter. In Colchester, elections were rigged from time to time by the sale of existing freedoms or the creation of new ones, but generally an election there was a fair

James Keir Hardie

81

indication of popular opinion. In Maldon, the 'Cockpit of Essex', elections down to just over 100 years ago were corrupt and disorderly. The notorious election of 1826 cost the three candidates nearly £50,000. The poll was open daily from 7 June to 23 June, but the mayor closed it early on days when Whig supporters were known to be coming from London, though he kept it open beyond the appointed time when Tory electors were on their way. He even left his place on the hustings and went into the polling booth to influence the voters.

The Reform Act of 1832 abolished 143 of the worst 'pocket' and 'rotten' boroughs in the country and gave the seats to larger towns and heavily populated counties; but it brought few changes for Essex. The county was split into two divisions, each with two members; the three ancient boroughs still returned two members each, though more people in them were given the vote. By the Act of 1867, the county was divided into three areas, each with two members. Colchester retained its two members, but Maldon and Harwich each lost one. After the Act of 1884, eight one-member county divisions were set up; Colchester lost one member; Maldon and Harwich were merged into the county divisions bearing their name; West Ham was given two members. By the Act of 1918, there were drastic changes to give fairer representation to the large and rapidly-growing population of the south-west. There were still eight parliamentary divisions, but their boundaries were greatly altered. West Ham's representation was raised to four. East Ham, Leyton, and Walthamstow were each given two members, and Ilford and Southend one apiece. Colchester borough was merged into the Colchester parliamentary division. In recent years, the outer rim of London-over-the-Border has been growing while places nearer the centre have declined in population. Meanwhile, in the rest of the county the numbers of the electorate have been rising. These trends were reflected in changes made in 1945, 1948 and 1955: the county constituencies were raised to 10; the county boroughs of Southend, East Ham and West Ham, and the boroughs of Walthamstow and Ilford were each divided into two single-member constituencies, while Leyton, Woodford, Barking, Dagenham, Romford and Hornchurch returned one member apiece.

A major revision of parliamentary representation, made by an Order of 1970, came into operation in 1974; this is shown on the map. Within the present administrative county there are still 10 county divisions each returning one member, but many of their boundaries are very different from those established in the 1940s and 1950s. In addition there are four one-member borough constituencies. Equally radical changes were made in the former Essex metropolitan boroughs, now all part of Greater London. Newham (formerly East Ham and

82

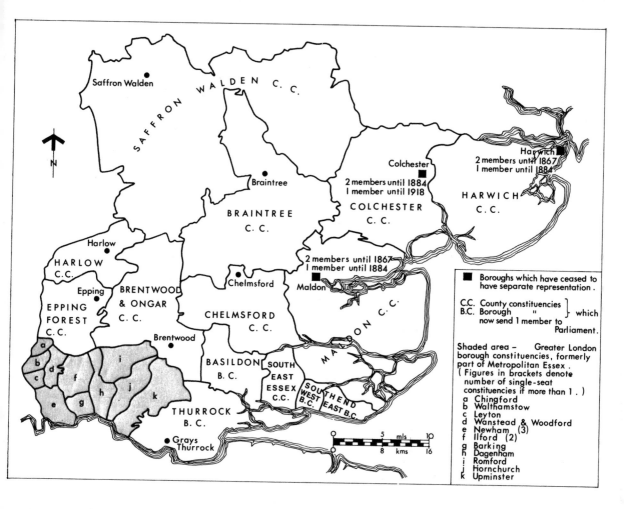

West Ham) now has three one-member constituencies; Ilford has two; the other nine return one member apiece.

Over the past century or so, there have been changes in the franchise and in the conduct of elections. The Ballot Act of 1870, which established secret voting, and the first effective Corrupt Practices Act of 1883 put an end to the widespread bribery and corruption at elections. The various reform acts steadily widened the franchise, so that by 1928 every man and woman in Britain who was not a peer, a foreigner, a certified lunatic, or a criminal in prison, had a vote. The growth of democracy led, almost inevitably, to the rise of a third political party, the Labour party. In 1892, West Ham South returned James Keir Hardie as the first Labour member of parliament in Britain. He went to take his seat wearing a tweed cap and was accompanied to Westminster by a brass band.

FURTHER READING

Victoria County History, Vol. II, pp. 242-52.

A. F. J. Brown, *English History from Essex Sources, 1750-1900,* pp. 183-210.

N. Rowley, *Essex Elections and the Great Reform Bill.* Seax Series, 8.

XII Early Roads and Improved Waterways

When the East Saxon invaders settled down in small communities or isolated homesteads, they seldom used the straight, well-planned and well-built Roman roads, many of which became overgrown and forgotten. Gradually they and their descendants built up a new pattern of 'ways' that are now 'the crooked by-roads, the bridle-paths and footpaths which baffle the modern stranger in rural Essex'—ways which led to mill and river, to church and market, from farm to farm and from village to village, winding around the boundaries of fields enclosed direct from Royal Forest long before the earliest surviving records.

Will Kemp, dancing from London to Norwich

All through the Middle Ages, the roads of Essex were hazardous and primitive, for it was difficult to enforce their maintenance. After the Highways Act of 1555, there was some improvement, for every parish had to elect its two surveyors of the highways and all parish householders had to work themselves or send labourers to repair the roads on four appointed days of the year. Wheeled traffic, still cumbersome and unsprung, began to increase. Even in early March of 1590, the Great Essex Road was firm enough for Dorothy Wadham to travel from Ingatestone to London in Lady Petre's coach. Regular carriers' services were also established: Jones of Romford would take the runlets of Malmsey from Aldgate to Romford, to be picked up by old John Exeter, the Shenfield carrier, and delivered to the Petre cellars. Nevertheless, for nearly another two centuries, the only reasonably comfortable way to travel was on horseback.

In 1696, the first turnpike gate in Essex was set up by Act of Parliament across the highway at Mountnessing. At first it was controlled by the Essex magistrates, and the tolls which were charged went to the upkeep of five widely-separated stretches of Essex road. Later, this first turnpike venture became an independent trust, known as the Essex Trust. During the 18th century it steadily took over and turnpiked roads in the north, centre and south of the county, including the main road from Shenfield to Colchester. The Middlesex and Essex Trust, established in 1722, took over roads in south-west Essex. The Epping and Ongar Trust was founded by an Act of 1703. The Essex and Herts Trust took over the road from Harlow to the north Essex boundary. In the very south of the county, where the need for road improvement was greatest on account of the traffic congestion and road damage caused by chalk waggons from Purfleet, there was little done until after 1793.

These independent Trusts were not without their faults and disadvantages. They depended on tolls and had no power to raise rates; thus their cash flow was uncertain and they were often obliged to borrow heavily. There was no clear division between their roles and those of the parish surveyors who were still responsible for enforcing the old statute labour and still answerable to the justices for their actions. The trusts were originally intended to be a short-term solution to the problem of maintaining good roads, but they lingered on, often in debt, and when they did fade out they left a tangle of legal troubles for the statutory authorities, including Highway Boards and County Councils, which took over their functions in the later part of the 19th century.

But they did succeed, on the whole, in improving and maintaining the roads in Essex, and in some parts of the county there was also an improvement in roads which were not turnpiked. The result was an increase in the quantity, quality and speed of vehicles, especially when some of the main roads were 'macadamised' under the guidance of Sir James McAdam, son of the famous John Loudon McAdam. The towns of Essex and East Anglia were linked to one another and to London by coach services. In 1785, the first Royal Mail coaches ran in Essex. The demand for more and more private coaches and carriages and a great variety of lighter well-sprung vehicles brought the crafts of the coach-builder and the wheelwright to their highest point of perfection and prosperity in the years between 1820 and 1840. Soon, however, this busy traffic dwindled with the development and popularity of the railways, and the highways and byways of Essex did not awake again until the coming of the motor-car in the present century.

Virtually nothing is known about the maintenance of Essex inland waterways during the Middle Ages. Maybe, little was needed: Essex rivers above their tidal estuaries probably flowed appreciably faster and were less liable to silting than today. Certainly they were *used*, especially for transporting heavy loads which would have been stuck axle deep on the roads; the Barnack stone facings for Hedingham's massive Norman keep probably came by river from the quarries to the Wash, then around the coast, and then up the River Colne.

'Double' mile-post at Mountnessing

Later, from the late 17th century onwards, when improved communications became more urgently needed, the large and important undertakings were directed towards improving existing rivers. Indeed, as John Booker has pointed out, there are some significant points of similarity between navigations and turnpikes. Both took over

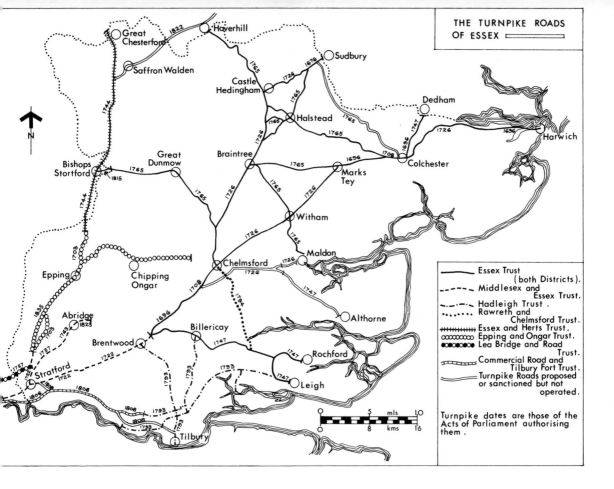

The Turnpike Roads of Essex

existing or potential lines of communications, both were run by bodies empowered to collect tolls; all turnpike trusts before 1820 and many navigation undertakers operated largely outside the administrative control of the Quarter Sessions.

The first recorded project of any importance was the improvement of the Lea, which was made navigable up to Ware from 1571. The plan to make the Stort navigable from the Lea to Bishops Stortford was achieved by 1769; but attempts to extend it farther were blocked by Lord Howard de Walden, who felt it would spoil the amenities of his mansion and park at Audley End. This meant that a grand scheme to link the Thames and the Wash by way of the Cam was never carried out. The improvement of the Colne from Colchester to Wivenhoe followed Acts passed in 1623, 1690 and 1725, but this hardly counts as an inland waterway as it is a tidal stretch of the river. The Stour navigation between Manningtree and Sudbury was an early 18th-century venture which remained workable until the First World War. There were relatively minor schemes to improve the Essex rivers

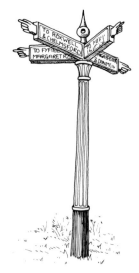
Finger-post, Good Easter

flowing into the Thames—the Roding, the Bean, the Ingrebourne, and the Mardyke—and some of these were partially achieved. An even smaller scheme was a mile-long canal from the Blackwater to White House Farm at Mundon; this was a real canal, an artificially-cut channel.

Perhaps the most important achievement was the Chelmer and Blackwater Navigation. It was a waterway needed by the vigorous and thriving county town of Chelmsford in the late-17th century, but opposition by the borough of Maldon and the owners of land flanking the Chelmer postponed it for over 100 years. Then, a navigation carried out by Richard Coates under the general supervision of the eminent John Rennie was completed in 1797. It ran from Springfield Basin to Heybridge Basin, nearly 14 miles, and flourished until, like other navigations in Essex and elsewhere, it met severe competition from the coming and expansion of the railways. Today, it has a new role as an attractive waterway for the pleasures of cruising.

FURTHER READING

John Holmes and K. C. Newton, *Highways and Byways of Essex.*
K. C. Newton, *Highways and Byways of Essex,* Seax Series, No. 1.
John Booker, *Essex and the Industrial Revolution.*
Peter Came, *A History of the Chelmer and Blackwater Navigation Canal.*
J. H. Boyes, *Waterways of Eastern England.*

XIII The Coming of the Railway

At first, only a relatively few people were interested in the early development of steam locomotion. Then, in 1829, came the opening of the Liverpool–Manchester Railway. George Stephenson's triumph over immense difficulties in building the line and the victory of his *Rocket* in the contest between the locomotives stirred the imagination of the public. Business men realised that a more powerful and rapid form of transport was now possible. Within the next 25 years, most of the main lines were built, and a constantly increasing network of railways was covering the country.

The first Essex railway projects gave the county its two main lines. In 1836, an Act of Parliament authorised the Eastern Counties Company to build a line running diagonally through the county to Colchester and Norwich. In the same year, another Act enabled the Northern and Eastern Company to construct a railway from London to Cambridge along the west Essex border. The Cambridge line reached Bishop's Stortford in 1842. It was taken over by the Eastern Counties in 1844. The new board resumed construction work: the line crossed the north-west corner of Essex a year later and linked up with the new railways serving the Fens and West Norfolk.

The Colchester line had to face greater problems. The early constructional costs were high: a long viaduct had to be built at its London end, and the difficulties of crossing the marshes between Bow and Stratford were greater than had been allowed for in the estimates. Many landowners went to law, unsuccessfully, to oppose the passage of railways through their lands. Most of them were consoled by heavy compensation: Lord Petre demanded and received £120,000, and used part of it to buy an estate in the Dengie Hundred. Indeed, the line cost the Eastern Counties about £57,000 a mile to construct. It reached Brentwood in 1840, Chelmsford in 1842, and Colchester in May 1843. It brought increased prosperity: in Chelmsford, for instance, the population grew by nearly 24 per cent. between 1841 and 1861; the market became one of the busiest in Essex, and the transport facilities were all ready for the considerable industrial development later in the century.

Many railway schemes followed. Some were begun and abandoned: very little of the Mistley, Thorpe and Walton line was built, and the project is mainly remembered for a stand-up fight between the original

Electric train, Southend Pier, 1889

89

*On the revived
Stour Valley Line*

contractor's navvies and a group of longshore men, or 'lumpers', hired by his successor to expel him; the 'lumpers' won! Some schemes were successfully completed or partially completed. A great deal depended on the attitude of the Eastern Counties Railway, never very sound financially, but always powerful because it was the first in the field and occupied a key position geographically. If it promoted a large scheme, like the London, Tilbury and Southend Railway, the project would be completed in a reasonable time. Sometimes it would promise branch lines and then fail to build them, but would vigorously obstruct any independent company which attempted to take up the project, such as the Colne Valley Railway. This was characteristic of the infighting in early railway politics—and characteristic, too, of the formidable George Hudson, the 'Railway King', who was brought in as chairman in 1845 to save the Eastern Counties from financial ruin. Moreover, the ordinary, day-to-day running of the company was inefficient: the rates were too high; the trains were unpunctual, too few in number, and badly time-tabled.

The Eastern Counties originally intended to extend their trans-Essex railway from Colchester to Norwich, but this became financially impossible even before the line reached Colchester. However, they managed to link up with Norwich through their Northern and Eastern line to Cambridge and beyond. The Colchester–Norwich link was eventually achieved by the Eastern Union Railway. The first stretch, from Colchester to Ipswich was opened in 1846; the Eastern Counties was most co-operative, but later became obstructive when the Eastern· Union extended their line to Norwich. However, the Eastern Counties' reign of intrigue, obstruction, inefficiency and financial instability came to an end in 1862, when it was merged with the newly-created Great Eastern Railway. From its beginning, the Great Eastern was wisely directed, indeed, for a short while it had as chairman a future prime minister in Lord Cranborne, later the renowned Marquis of Salisbury.

All other Essex railways may be regarded as branches of the Eastern Counties, or the Great Eastern, even if they were not originally promoted by them. Most of them were completed by the end of the century; all except a few minor lines are shown on the map. Several were remarkable. The London, Tilbury and Southend Railway was promoted jointly in 1852 by the Eastern Counties and the London and Blackwall, but 10 years later it managed to gain a precarious independence and maintain it until 1921. It was built originally to carry Londoners to Tilbury, where they would then take the ferry to the pleasure gardens near Gravesend; the promoters also hoped for large-scale traffic from Thames Haven. But it was the rapid growth

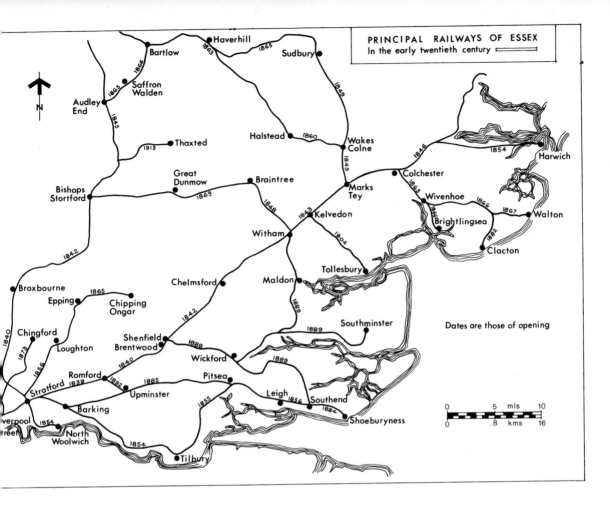

of Southend which brought it most prosperity. Its fares were low, its trains were punctual, and its far-sighted management was usually a step ahead of the powerful Great Eastern in the provision of branches, particularly the Romford-Pitsea link on the Southend line.

Essex branch lines were, of course, commercial ventures—for the bulk transport of agricultural produce, for serving the industries of Essex towns (some of them remote), for taking holidaymakers to the seaside and Continental travellers to and from Harwich, for carrying the London commuter service. But some of them are deeply etched in the memory for other reasons. On the Stour Valley line, it was possible to cross the Chappel viaduct, 1,066ft. long, with 32 arches, the most imposing Victorian architectural monument in the county, and then amble gently along the delightful Essex–Suffolk border. There was the Witham–Maldon branch where the porters spoke pure Essex and not Cockney dialect; and a bridge over the line was affectionately known as 'Langford Hill'. There was the waterside run to Brightlingsea,

91

with its passage over the swaying Alresford swing-bridge. There was the long, straight switchback line from Braintree to Bishop's Stortford, running parallel with the ancient Stane Street. Moreover, with ingenuity and a little patience it was possible to go by rail from Essex villages to any part of Britain without going to London; indeed, in the Second World War, when the V1s and V2s were falling on the capital, one Yorkshire lady, prudent rather than timid, enjoyed her roundabout journeys between mid-Essex and the West Riding!

FURTHER READING

D. I. Gordon, *A Regional History of the Railways of Great Britain,* Vol. 5—*Eastern Counties.*
E. J. Allen, *The Great Eastern Railway.*
J. Oxley-Parker, *The Oxley-Parker Papers,* Chapter 12.
There are a number of booklets on individual Essex railways.

Early train crossing Stratford Marshes

XIV The Seaboard of Essex

Strangers do not immediately think of Essex as a maritime county, but, in fact, no other county, except perhaps Kent, has had its history moulded so firmly by the sea and by the rivers which flow into it. As William Camden pointed out in Elizabethan times, Essex is almost surrounded by water: by the Stour in the north, by the North Sea in the east, by the Thames estuary in the south, and by the Lea and the Stort in the west. All successive waves of prehistoric invaders down to the early Iron Age landed on its coast, and they and later invaders travelled by the Essex tidal estuaries and river valleys when they penetrated farther into the country. In more modern times, it has continued as a vulnerable gateway, to be guarded closely when danger threatened. In 1588, Leicester's army waited at Tilbury for the outcome of the naval encounter in the Channel. In the Napoleonic Wars and in 1940, the citizen armies kept an anxious and unremitting watch on the Essex coast against invaders who were never able to gain the vital control of the Narrow Seas.

Gatehouse,
Tilbury Fort

Essex, like all maritime counties, has had to fight the most remorseless invader of all, the sea. In the north-east, the frontal attack on the cliffs of Walton, Frinton and Clacton has been severe. The site of Walton parish church which disappeared in 1798 is now well out to sea; and it has taken all the skill of modern engineering to check the rate of erosion. Elsewhere, the problem is even graver, for the foreshore is not only low-lying but is also steadily sinking—it is, perhaps, 12 or 13ft. lower than in Roman times. By the end of the 12th century, Essex men were being forced to embank the coast to prevent flooding. Each landlord or tenant was responsible for maintaining his own stretch of sea-wall and scouring his own ditches, but, from time to time, kings appointed special 'commissioners of walls and ditches' to see that the work was being carried out. In 1531, Henry VIII's Statute of Sewers finally established the regular appointment of Commissioners of Sewers, and, for over three centuries, the Essex coastal areas were divided into a number of 'levels', each holding its own court. This work is now the responsibility of the Essex River Division, which has over 300 miles of sea-walls under its control. On these walls depend the safety of thousands of lives, thousands of acres, and millions of pounds'-worth of industrial plant. Collapse of the defences can lead to disaster. This has happened on many occasions. The Dagenham

Dutch Cottage, Canvey Island

Breach of 1707, for instance, was looked upon as a great calamity, but it was utterly dwarfed by the catastrophe of February 1953, when a spring tide, swollen and driven by a hurricane, overwhelmed the defences at points all round the Essex coast from Manningtree to West Ham, engulfed huge areas, including Harwich, Jaywick, Canvey Island, Tilbury, and Purfleet, drowned about 100 people, and left over 21,000 homeless. Sometimes Essex has taken the offensive. Canvey Island was won from the sea through the enterprise of Sir Henry Appleton, the Cavalier, and the financial backing of the Dutchman, Joas Croppenburg.

Until modern times, the Essex coast has been remote and thinly populated, for behind the sea-walls there is amost continuous marshland from Bow Creek to Mersea. In the past, this made good summer pasture for sheep, and produced, said Camden, 'cheeses of uncommon size, which are sent, not only over England, but abroad, for the use of the peasants and labourers'. Camden and other historians emphasise the unhealthiness of the marshlands, where, according to Defoe, writing in 1724, the ague, or malaria, was more fatal to women than to men, so that 'it was very frequent to meet with men who had had from five or six to fourteen or fifteen wives'. Only where there were good anchorages backed by rising ground, as at Leigh, Brightlingsea and Harwich, or at the heads of estuaries, as at Rochford, Maldon, Colchester and Mistley, could ports grow up and flourish (see Chapter V). In the 18th century, however, before the coming of railways and good secondary roads, the coastal trade with London had become so great that almost any 'hard' on a navigable creek was used for wharfage.

Although so much of the seaboard remained remote, it was not deserted or inactive. The lonely 'wallers', maintaining the dykes, could see the coastal traders passing by and the fishermen crossing to Terschelling or off to more distant fishing grounds. In the river estuaries, the valuable oyster-layings were carefully tended and jealously guarded. Wild-fowling was a flourishing enterprise, as the decoy ponds, scattered along the coast from Hamford Water to Paglesham, testify. There were 31 in all, more than in any county except Lincolnshire. By far the most profitable and widespread marshland activity was smuggling. Around 1800, the entire population of Paglesham was engaged in this 'free trade'. In one year they smuggled in 13,476 gallons of geneva and brandy, and £200-worth of silk at a time was hidden in three hollow elms near East Hall. The most famous Paglesham smuggler was 'Hard Apple' Blyth, churchwarden and grocer, who wrapped up the butter and bacon in pages torn from the parish registers. In their 'spare' time, he and his crew of smugglers often played cricket in the field near the *Punch Bowl* inn, taking care to place their cutlasses and loaded pistols in readiness on their jackets.

For many hundreds of years, only the sea itself wrought any change on remote stretches of the Essex seaboard. Then, in the 18th century, doctors recommended the medical benefits of sea-bathing, and the English nation began to discover the pleasures of the seaside. Margate, Brighton and Weymouth were all well established before a determined effort was made in the 1790s to develop the South End of Prittlewell as the first Essex seaside resort. On the cliffs above the existing hamlet, the Terrace and the *Grand* hotel, with its Assembly Room, were built, the Shrubbery was laid out and the covered sea-water baths, named after Caroline, Princess of Wales, were opened. In 1803, the Princess spent three months at the Terrace, and this, more than anything else, helped to establish Southend as 'a watering-place of fashion and reputation', where 'the lower orders of the community have hitherto found little inducement to intrude'. For another 50 years, Southend developed slowly and steadily, and remained largely a resort for Essex county families and fashionable people from London. After 1856, when the London, Tilbury and Southend Railway was completed, the growth of modern Southend began.

Walton-on-the-Naze was just beginning to emerge as a watering-place at the end of the Georgian period. The *Portobello* hotel was built in 1829, when bathing machines were already available on the beach; and within a few years terrace houses were built in a style intended to attract genteel visitors. Like Southend and like its much newer neighbours, Frinton and Clacton, Walton's development as a popular resort belongs to the story of the past 100 years (see Chapter XV).

Queen Victoria, Southend

FURTHER READING

P. Benton, *History of the Rochford Hundred.*
Hilda Grieve, *The Great Tide.*
W. Pollitt, *Southend, 1760–1860.*
W. Addison, *Thames Estuary.*
K. C. Newton, *Essex and the Sea,* revised 1970, by J. R. Smith.

XV The Latest Age

Crompton electric radiator, c. 1900

In the past century and a half, the history of Essex and its people has been deeply affected by the changing fortunes of agriculture and the outward spread of London.

The late Georgian period was a time of acute distress in agriculture (see Chapter X). From early Victorian times, British commerce and industry began to expand and prosper again at a time when war and revolution on the Continent delayed the rise of foreign competitors. This prosperity spread to agriculture. The rising population of London and other towns needed more food and had more money to pay for it. Better farming methods came with increased scientific knowledge; for instance, artificial fertilisers, such as superphosphates, and imported manures, like Peruvian guano, became more widely known and used. Men like J. J. Mechi of Tiptree Hall showed Essex farmers how to farm scientifically and profitably. The result, from 1853-1862, was a period of prosperity which rivalled the golden age of farming in the 18th century.

After 1862 there was a slight decline, and from 1874 there was a long period of depression. A series of bad harvests came at a time when the English market was being flooded with wheat from the prairie lands and refrigerated meat from America, the Argentine, and New Zealand. In Essex, the effects were disastrous. Scores of farms went out of cultivation. Rents fell rapidly. Shoats and Canny Farms at Steeple, 638 acres in all, were let in 1873 for £760 a year, the tenant also paying a tithe of £140. In 1883, the rent was £460; in 1886, it was £1. Landlords, farmers and farm workers slowly came to realise that the land could no longer support so many people and that the costs of cultivation were too high. This was made clear by the success of Scotsmen from the dairylands of Renfrew and Ayrshire, who emigrated to the derelict farms of Essex and managed only by unremitting labour and the strictest economies to win a livelihood from the land. These immigrants by no means made up for the drift from the country to Metropolitan Essex, but they set an example—a hard one, but the only way to follow for the next 25 years. There was a steady improvement at the beginning of the present century, so that a visitor to Essex in 1913 could report that 'the countryside seemed to smile with a quiet, unexcited prosperity—it was providing bread and butter, at all events, for its occupiers'.

96

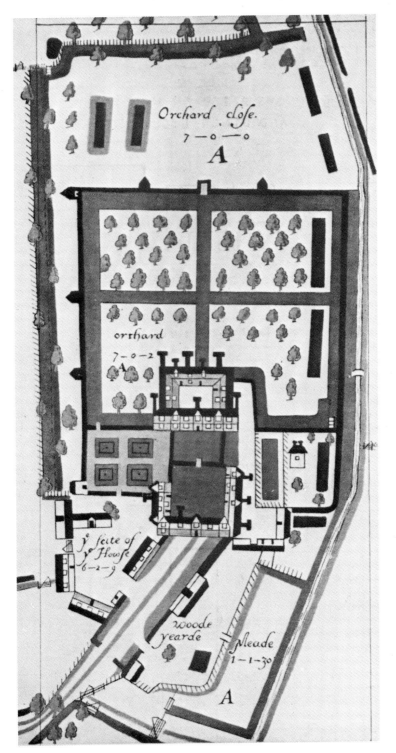

Orchard close.
7 — 0 — 0
A

orchard
7 — 0 — 2
A

y^e scite of
y^e Howse
6 — 2 — 9

woode
yearde

Meade
1 — 1 — 3°

A

23. Plan of Ingatestone Hall, redrawn from Walker's map of 1605

24. Bower Hall, Steeple Bumpstead, in its early 18th century setting. The house was demolished in 1996.

25. Audley End, the vast Jacobean palace of the Earls of Suffolk, was reduced in size in the 18th century. Its interior was remodelled by Vanbrugh and Robert Adam, and its grounds were landscaped by Capability Brown

26. Thorndon Hall, a Georgian mansion in the grand manner, was built by James Paine for the 9th Lord Petre in 1770

HIC IACET SAM = VELL HARSNETT

QVONDAM VICARIVS HVIVS ECCLESIÆ PRIMO

INDIGNVS EPISCOPVS CICESTRIENSIS DEINDIG

NIOR EPISCOP⁹ NORWICENSIS⁼

DEMVM INDIGNISSIM⁹ ARCHIEPISCOP⁹ EBORACĒN

QVI OBIJT XXV DIE MAIJ ANNO DÑI· 1631·

QVOD IPSISSIMVM EPITAPHIVM EX ABVNDANTI
HVMILITATE SIBI PONI TESTAMENTO CVRAVIT
REVERENDISSIMVS PRÆSVL

27. Brass of Archbishop Harsnett, d. 1631, who founded Chigwell
School

Not until the middle of the First World War did the government fully realise the seriousness of the German submarine menace and the desperate need to grow more food to avert defeat by starvation. The national effort was directed to bringing over 2½ million acres under the plough. The farmer was guaranteed prices for his wheat, and wages boards were set up to fix a minimum wage and regulate hours of work for farm labourers. After the war, it seemed for a while that, at last, farming in peace-time would receive the support and encouragement it needed from the state; but in 1921, the plans were abandoned, the slump set in once more, and for some years much of the wheatland of Essex became merely rough pasture. From the mid–1920s some government assistance was given—wages boards were brought back, wheat was subsidised, agricultural land was de-rated, sugar-beet cultivation was encouraged, and a sugar-beet factory was set up at Felsted. Farming in Essex, as elsewhere, recovered from the slump, but the countryside languished through lack of a national policy for agriculture.

This policy the Second World War supplied. Working through War Agricultural Committees, the government acted promptly and drew upon the agricultural experience of the previous war. After 1945, the lesson was remembered. A peace-time agricultural policy has to be more flexible than a war-time one. Indirect control still remained— by varying the subsidies and prices the government made it profitable for the farmer to raise more of those products which happened to be most needed nationally at any one time. In return, the farmer had his guaranteed prices, he knew where he stood and could plan ahead. This policy is now being changed as a result of Britain's entry into the European Community, but it is unlikely that the *standard* of farming will be affected. Indeed, for 30 years or more, Essex has been as well farmed as it was in Arthur Young's time. Wheat, for which the county was famous as long ago as pre-Roman times, is firmly back again; but it has not pushed out the other cereals, the good dairy farming and grazing, the sugar beet and peas, the extensive fruit farms producing high quality apples, the seed-growing industry, and the market garden-ing in the Lea Valley and in the brick-earth lands backing the coastal marshes.

Early in the 19th century, London was beginning to cross the Essex border. In 1801, West Ham's population was 6,500, and Leytonstone and Walthamsow were becoming large villages; even so, only 14,000 of the county's population of 228,000 lived in the whole of south-west Essex. With the coming of the railways, however, the rate of spread increased, so that by 1901 over half the population of the geographical county lived in West Ham, East Ham and Metropolitan Essex. In the

Crompton electric urn, c. 1900

*Shell refinery,
Thameshaven*

past seven decades, the spread has continued in the same remorseless way. In the north it extends well beyond Loughton. It has moved eastwards far along the Thames. It has stretched north-eastwards along the Great Essex Road almost to Brentwood. This is not all—London has penetrated more deeply into Essex, for Harlow in the north, Southend and Canvey on the east, and even Frinton in the far north-east may partly be regarded as its outliers.

The reasons for London's spread are complicated and difficult to disentangle. Its commerce and industry have not been able to find room enough for expansion within its own boundaries and about 100 years ago began to move outwards, especially along the Thames. Larger docks were needed for larger ships: the Royal Victoria Dock was built in 1855, followed by the Royal Albert and the Tilbury Docks in the 1880s, and the George V Dock in 1921. The great cement manufacturing industry developed in the Purfleet area from the 1870s. The first American oil came to Thames Haven as far back as 1880. Today the marshlands of Canvey Island, Shell Haven, Thames Haven and Coryton are covered with methane and oil storage and oil refinery plant on which the traffic and industry of London and south-eastern England depend. Between the World Wars, when there was depression in the industrial areas of the North, important industries sprang up in Metropolitan Essex where prospects for trade were greater, and costs of transport were less. Many of these, notably the Ford Motor industry and its allied companies at Dagenham, were established on the banks of the Thames where there were deep anchorages. All this—the extensive docks, a score of important industries from heavy engineering and chemicals to electrical, concrete and asbestos products, and many lesser industries—has acted like a magnet. People moved out from Inner London; people moved in from agricultural Essex, and from outside the county.

Other people moved from London to Essex for a very different reason—to get away from its crowded conditions and its smoke and noise. In mid-Victorian times, middle-class people made their homes in places like Woodford, Buckhurst Hill and Romford (the town centre, and, later, Gidea Park). The head of the household then travelled daily by train to his work in town, while his family lived in surroundings which remained semi-rural until London began to catch up with them again. In the past 50 years, this outward movement has been aided by the expansion of bus services, the production of cheaper cars (until inflation became rampant!), and the general rise in prosperity. Seaside resorts, and, to a less extent, distant rural areas have also attracted people from Metropolitan Essex and Inner London. True, seaside resorts owe a good deal of their prosperity to holidaymakers; but there

98

are also many people for whom the seaside or countryside has become a temporary or permanent home. Southend and Walton, whose origins go back to Georgian times, Clacton, dating from the mid-Victorian age, Frinton, a 20th-century resort, all have a resident population, drawn originally from London and not connected with the holiday industry. Other people, usually with rather less money, have built houses or bungalows on Canvey Island, at Jaywick, or at smaller places dotted along the river estuaries or in rural districts. Again a small, but rapidly increasing number of people, many of them from the metropolitan area, have permanent or temporary homes at the yachting and boat-building town of Burnham-on-Crouch and at other maritime places, where they can follow their interest in sailing.

Another main reason for the spread of the capital into Essex was the London County Council's ever-pressing need to relieve its own congested areas. Its first great enterprise was the Becontree estate for 100,000 people, completed in 1932. A second smaller estate was begun just before the Second World War at Friday Hill, Chingford. By 1952, about 60,000 Londoners had already moved to the post-war housing estates at Debden, Hainault, and Harold Hill, and many to the estate of Aveley. The County Borough of East Ham had similar re-housing difficulties and built an estate at Ingrave.

Expansion has brought many problems. As the years roll by and the built-up areas spread, it becomes more difficult and costly to meet the need for improved railways and roads to handle the volume of goods, and carry more people to and from their work. The principal railway lines were laid down by 1882. The only important later additions are the direct line to Southend *via* Upminster, and the line from Shenfield to Southend. To carry the increasing number of passengers during the peak hours, the suburban railway system has been expanded and electrified during the past 50 years, and this was followed by the electrification of the main lines leading out from Metropolitan Essex. The congestion on the roads is serious and would have been worse if improvements had not been carried out between the World Wars. The trunk roads to Norwich, Colchester and Tilbury Docks were partly re-modelled and the North Circular Road, Eastern Avenue and the Southend Arterial Road were built. More recent road improvements have been considerable and some are still in progress, notably the M11 motorway. These changes are shown on the map.

It becomes equally difficult and expensive to supply the many other needs of an expanding population—water, gas, electricity, sewerage, and refuse disposal, as well as hospitals, schools, community centres, playing fields, and open spaces. For example, the size of the Barking power station or Beckton gasworks (formerly the largest in the world,

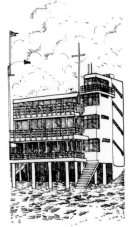

Royal Corinthian Yacht Club, Burnham-on-Crouch

but no longer producing town gas), gives some idea of the enormous initial cost of these services. The supply of water is limited by the rainfall, and Essex, with an annual average of 23.5ins., has the lowest rainfall of any county except Huntingdonshire. However, the existing sources, notably the Ely-Ouse Scheme and the provision of large reservoirs at Abberton and Hanningfield, have ensured enough water to supply a population of nearly two million. As the population of the county will almost certainly decline towards the end of the century, the water supply is not likely to become precarious. Some of the problems which confront modern planners are being solved by the advance of science; for instance, large supplies of electricity are now being fed into the national grid by the conventional power stations in Essex and, since 1963, by the nuclear generating station on its remote site at Bradwell, near St. Cedd's chapel of St. Peter.

For over a century it has been recognised that only an expanding public educational system could meet the needs of an expanding and mainly urban population. The system has been shaped and developed by various Acts from 1870 onwards. This has made for uniformity: public education in Essex, with some exceptions, has not been markedly different from public education in any other county. However, since the County Council assumed the main responsibility for education in 1902, Essex has generally been to the fore. In the inter-War period, Middlesex was regarded as the leading educational authority. In the years immediately following the Second World War, it was closely challenged by Essex and three or four other counties. Essex has long had a good reputation for the quality and design of its new schools and colleges; it has assiduously fostered further education, particularly technical education; it has been far-sighted in developing ancillary services, for example, its Visual and Aural Aids department. Like all authorities, it finds its educational practices are being transformed by modern educational policy, on which future generations will sit in judgment.

London's rate of spread into Essex has not always been even, and it was considerably checked during the World Wars. The large armies and the severe casualties of the years 1914–18 drained the manpower of the county, and all building was brought to a standstill. Essex, and especially Metropolitan Essex, had its first attacks from the air, but the destruction of life and property was slight. In the Second World War all building again ceased, and bombing brought heavy destruction. Essex experienced all forms of aerial attack—the early small-scale raids, the daylight bombing during the Battle of Britain, the long night attacks, the V1 and the V2. The whole county suffered, but the brunt fell on London, including Metropolitan Essex. In West Ham alone

Boiler house, c. 1933, Barking Power Station

100

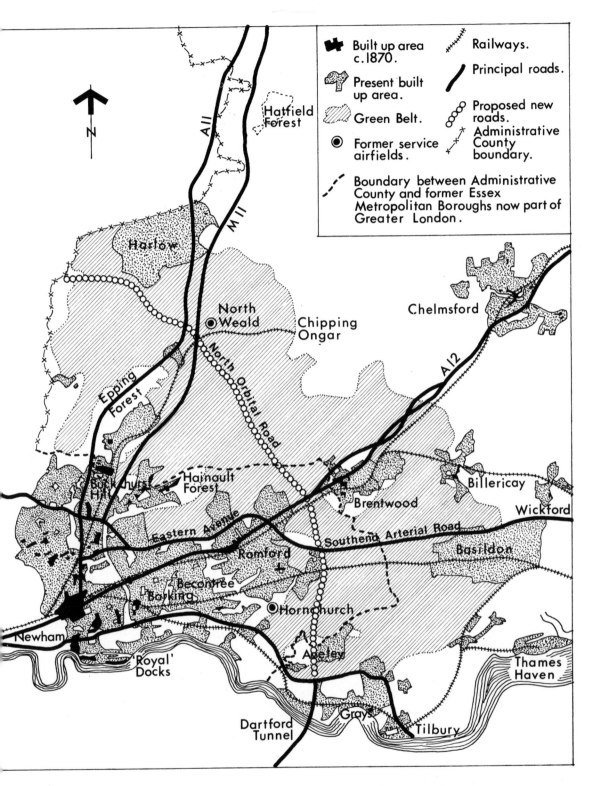

Built up area c.1870.

Present built up area.

Green Belt.

Former service airfields.

Railways.

Principal roads.

Proposed new roads.

Administrative County boundary.

Boundary between Administrative County and former Essex Metropolitan Boroughs now part of Greater London.

All

M II

Hatfield Forest

Harlow

North Weald

Chipping Ongar

Chelmsford

North Orbital Road

Epping Forest

A12

Buckhurst Hill

Hainault Forest

Brentwood

Billericay

Wickford

Eastern Avenue

Southend Arterial Road

Basildon

Romford

Beccontree

Barking

Hornchurch

Newham

'Royal' Docks

Aveley

Grays

Tilbury

Thames Haven

Dartford Tunnel

Town Hall, Colchester

14,000 houses were totally destroyed, 1,207 people were killed, and 6,500 were injured. Essex air bases became world-famous during the Battle of Britain. Fighter Command pilots from Hornchurch, Debden, Rochford and North Weald took a leading part in the defeat of the Luftwaffe. Later, when the Allies moved to the attack, R.A.F. and American bombers set out daily and nightly from the new airfields built across the northern half of the county.

The check to the expansion of London caused by the Second World War gave the Government, the Essex County Council and the Councils of the three County Boroughs an opportunity to draw up careful and detailed plans to regulate future spread. Most of these plans have now been carried out. A barrier of open country, about seven miles wide, surrounding the build-up area of Metropolitan Essex, has been designated as a Green Belt. The land has to be kept mainly for farming and recreation; no new industries are to be established on it and any other kind of building is strictly limited. Perhaps the most important government decision was the plan to transfer people and industries from Greater London either to existing towns or to the entirely 'New Towns' of Basildon and Harlow. The existing towns were those which already had industries established since later Victorian times on sites close to a railway, reasonably near a supply of labour and not too far from London, the main market and distributing centre. The most important of these was Chelmsford, noted for its ball-bearing and electrical industries and for the achievements of Marconi and his associates and successors. The New Towns were not meant to be mere collections of houses and factories, but real towns, planned down to the smallest detail before a single brick was laid, and timed, too, so that the building of houses, factories, schools and other services should keep pace with one another. Basildon was built partly on the site of a rural slum; the new Harlow has been skilfully woven into and around a small ancient town and three rural parishes. Both towns are now approaching a population of 80,000; neither is likely to grow much more. A good example of the care and ingenuity which has been shown was seen quite early, when The Stow, the shopping centre of the first neighbourhood area, was completed at Harlow. It is cheerful and compact; the essential shops are all there; people can look at the shop windows without getting wet in rainy weather; the centre was given a dance-hall, a post office, a branch of the county library and an inn. Even the inn-sign was thought out with care and humour; on one side is a bluff old salt, the *Essex Skipper*; on the other is a picture of the county's own special butterfly, the *Essex Skipper*.

The most radical change since the creation of the Essex County Council in 1889, came in 1965, when the independent County

Boroughs of East Ham and West Ham, the boroughs of Barking, Chingford, Dagenham, Ilford, Leyton, Romford, Walthamstow and Wanstead and Woodford, as well as Hornchurch and part of Chigwell, were all absorbed into Greater London. The population of the administrative county was reduced from 1,860,000 to 942,000, and the rateable value by more than half. An even more controversial change was made in 1974, when local government throughout the kingdom was reorganised. The 'two tier' system was introduced, by which 'Districts' were created by the amalgamation of smaller administrative units; there are 14 of these Districts in Essex. It is too early to judge the wisdom of these 1974 changes, but the impression remains with many who care deeply for Essex that central governments, whatever their political complexions and however worthy their intentions, do not fully understand the needs and problems of local government. Today, the population of Essex has risen again to 1,450,000, partly by the deliberately planned growth of towns, such as Chelmsford, and partly by the return of the former county borough of Southend to the administrative county.

To those who cherish the Essex past, it is comforting to realise that there are other powerful forces at work. For instance, there is the incomparable work of Women's Institutes in saving and fostering village life. For many years the numerous local historical and archaeological societies, together with the Essex Record Office, have actively promoted the study of the local past. More recently they have been reinforced by the work of the County Committee of the *Victoria County History* and its editor, and by local amenity societies whose interests lie not only in preservation but also in striving to combat the more garish intrusions of modernity. Even more recent is the realisation at government and local government levels of the need for conservation. In one notable respect, the Essex County Council is considered to be leading the way in Britain. Its Planning Department has set up an Environmental Branch served by expert officers charged with the duty of recording the archaeology of the county, preserving the Essex landscape and its unique heritage of ancient buildings, and planning to secure an ordered and pleasing environment for the future.

As long as people care enough and are vigilant, there is hope for the future of Essex—and for the preservation of its past. The first Henry Ford said, 'History is bunk', but even he came under its powerful spell. He *made* history at Dagenham. He tried to *remove* a piece of Essex history to America—'Bull's Lodge', Boreham, with its memories of Henry VIII and Anne Boleyn—but he did not get away with it!

FURTHER READING

Lord Ernle, *English Farming, Past and Present.*

A. F. J. Brown, *English History from Essex Sources, 1750–1900.*

R. G. E. Wood, *Agriculture in Essex,* c. *1840–1900.* Seax Series, No. 7.

Rider Haggard, *Rural England,* Vol. I.

J. Oxley-Parker, *The Oxley-Parker Papers.*

County of Essex Development Plan. 1952. The Report of the Survey.

John Booker, *Essex and the Industrial Revolution.*

Victoria County History, Vol. V (for introduction on Metropolitan Essex).

N. Rowley, *Town Life and Improvement in Essex, 1730-1908.* Seax Series, No. 5.

Abbey Mills Pumping Station, Stratford

XVI A Select Dictionary of Essex Biography

AUDLEY, Thomas, Baron Audley of Walden (1488-1544), was born at Earls Colne. He was appointed Town Clerk of Colchester in 1516, was returned to Parliament in 1523 and soon became prominent. In 1529, he was chosen Speaker of the Reformation Parliament which passed acts destroying the authority of the Pope over the English Church. He succeeded Sir Thomas More as Lord Chancellor to Henry VIII. It was he who sanctioned Henry's divorce from Katharine of Aragon and presided over the trials of More and Bishop Fisher. He was created Baron Audley of Walden in 1538 and was richly rewarded with spoils from the dissolution of the monasteries, among them the lands of Walden Abbey. He was buried in Saffron Walden church, where his monument still stands.

Thomas, Lord Audley

BALL, John (d. 1381), priest, and one of the leaders of the Peasants' Revolt, 1381, came from York to Colchester. His belief that all men should be equal made him a popular preacher with the north Essex villeins and brought him into trouble with the Church authorities. When the Peasants' Revolt broke out, the Kentish insurgents released him from the Archbishop's prison at Maidstone. At Blackheath he preached his famous sermon (see Chapter IV), calling on the peasants to overthrow the chief lords of the kingdom and all lawyers and set up a new commonwealth based on social equality. After the failure of the Revolt, he was executed at St. Albans. A sympathetic, imaginative account of his times is given in *A Dream of John Ball*, by William Morris (*q.v.*).

BARING-GOULD, Sabine (1834-1924), spent 10 years of his long and active life as rector of East Mersea, where he wrote *Mehalah*, a powerful novel of the marshlands.

BARNARDO, Thomas John (1845-1905), devoted his life to saving and caring for homeless children in an age when the public conscience was not yet awakened to their sufferings. His boys' home at Stepney devoloped into 'Dr. Barnardo's Homes', and he founded the 'Girls' Village Home', at Barkingside. He began his life's mission while still a medical student, and worked unremittingly all his life, seldom going to bed before three in the morning, in order to keep his vow—'No destitute child ever refused admission'.

BARRINGTON, Sir Thomas (d. 1644), was descended from an ancient Essex family of Hatfield Broad Oak. He sat as member for Newtown, Isle of Wight, in the last parliament of James I and the first three of Charles I and left an invaluable diary of the debates in 1621. He was the chief promoter of the venture to colonise the island of Providence in the Gulf of Mexico, 1631-41. He was returned for Essex in the Short Parliament and for Colchester in the Long Parliament, and supported his friend, John Pym, in his opposition to the king. He was one of those largely responsible for keeping Essex on Parliament's side during the Civil War.

BASTWICK, John (1593-1654), physician of Colchester, was born at Writtle and was educated at Emmanuel College, Cambridge, and Padua. In 1637, he was summoned before the Star Chamber for libelling the bishops, and was tried at the same time as William Prynne and Henry Burton. They were sentenced to lose their ears, to be fined £5,000, and to be imprisoned for life. In 1640, Bastwick was released by order of the Long Parliament.

BATE DUDLEY, Sir Henry (1745-1824), clergyman, journalist, magistrate and sportsman, was a friend of Mrs. Siddons, Garrick, Hogarth and Gainsborough, and was one of the early editors of the radical newspaper, the *Morning Post*. As Justice of the Peace in Essex and 10 other counties, he worked hard and successfully to bring about better roads. At Bradwell-juxta-Mare, he spent over £28,000 in draining marshes and making other agricultural improvements, and lived 'more as a squire than a parson' at Bradwell Lodge which John Johnson, the architect (*q.v.*), designed for him.

John Bastwick

BOURCHIER, Henry, Earl of Essex (d. 1483), of Little Easton, served in the French wars under the Duke of York, became Lord Treasurer of England, and fought on the Yorkist side in the Wars of the Roses. He and his wife, Isabella, aunt of Edward IV and Richard II, were buried at Beeleigh Abbey beneath a fine monument with brass effigies. When Beeleigh Abbey was dissolved in 1536, their bodies and tomb were removed to Little Easton church. (See p. 28)

BRAMSTON, Sir John, the elder (1577–1654), was born at Maldon. He was educated at the 'free schoole' there, and at Jesus College, Cambridge, and the Middle Temple. In 1635, the same year that he was appointed Lord Chief Justice, he bought Skreens at Roxwell, where his descendants lived for over 200 years. He was an ardent Royalist, whose life and times are vividly depicted in the *Autobiography* of his son, Sir John Bramston, the younger (1611–1700). His portrait, one of considerable merit, hangs in County Hall, Chelmsford.

Sir Henry Bate Dudley

BROWNE, Sir Anthony (1510–67), judge, of Weald Hall, was the son of Sir Wistan Browne of Abbess Roothing. In Mary's reign he was an active persecutor of Protestants, among them William Hunter, burnt at Brentwood, and George ('Trudge-over-the-World') Eagles, hanged at Chelmsford. He founded Brentwood School in 1558, and in the same year was appointed Chief Justice of the Common Pleas.

BUXTON, Sir Thomas Fowell (1786-1845), of Colne Place, Earls Colne, was descended from the Buxtons of Coggeshall, a family of clothiers. He was educated privately and at Trinity College, Dublin, and then he became a partner in the family brewing firm of Truman, Hanbury and Buxton. From 1818 to 1837 he served as M.P. for Weymouth, and with his friend, William Wilberforce, he worked for the abolition of slavery in British dominions; this was achieved in 1833. He was an advocate of penal reform: he visited the prisons with his sister-in-law, Elizabeth Fry (*q.v.*) and was himself largely responsible for the reduction of capital offences from 230 to nine.

BYRD, William (1540–1623), one of the greatest of English composers, was 'bred up to music under Thomas Tallis' (*q.v.*). He was a Roman Catholic, but his privileged position as a Gentleman of the Chapel Royal and his friendship with John, first Lord Petre, probably saved him and his family from serious persecution. He was a frequent visitor to the Petre household at Thorndon before he finally settled near by at Stondon Massey in 1593. His compositions covered the whole range of contemporary music—madrigals, solo-songs, canons, rounds, instrumental music for virginals and strings, and, above all, church music. His works for the Anglican Church include anthems and two complete services. For Roman Church services he composed three masses and two books of *Gradualia*, the second dedicated to Lord Petre.

107

CONSTABLE, John (1778–1837), was born at East Bergholt, just inside the Suffolk border, but Essex can justifiably claim a share of him: he was educated at Dedham Grammar School; at Dedham, too, he received valuable encouragement from Sir George Beaumont, the Essex patron of artists; and, of course, the Dedham Vale from Langham to Dedham, now so famous, was the scene of so many of his paintings. Among his other Essex works, his Wivenhoe Park and Hadleigh Castle are outstanding.

COOKE, Sir Anthony (1504–76), tutor to King Edward VI and politician, was the son of John Cooke of Gidea Hall. He was educated privately and acquired vast learning, much of which he passed on to his daughters and, incidentally, to Lady Jane Grey. A firm Protestant, he was forced to retire to Strasburg during Mary Tudor's reign, but returned on Elizabeth's accession. He was M.P. for Essex for nine years and an indefatigable 'committee-man', serving on a number of government commissions. He received Queen Elizabeth at Gidea Hall in 1568. He had four undistinguished sons and five daughters, of whom at least three were highly gifted; his eldest daughter, Mildred, became the second wife of William Cecil, Lord Burghley; his second daughter, Ann, was the mother of Francis Bacon. His handsome monument in Romford Church has recently been restored.

CRANFIELD, Lionel, Earl of Middlesex (1573–1645), made a fortune as a merchant adventurer. In 1613 he entered the service of James I. He applied his financial skill to the royal revenues and increased them by £30,000 within two years. He was knighted and became M.P. for Hythe and later for Arundel. In 1621, he was made Lord Treasurer, and in the following year he was created Earl of Middlesex. His application of strict economy and business methods to the finances brought him many enemies. In 1624, he was accused of taking bribes. He was sent to the Tower and fined £50,000, but was soon released and pardoned. He spent his last 20 years quietly on his estates at Copt Hall, Epping.

Lionel Cranfield,
Earl of Middlesex

CROMPTON, Colonel Rookes Evelyn Bell (1845–1940), at the age of 10, visited his brother in the trenches before Sebastopol and returned to England with the Crimean Medal and Sebastopol clasp. As a Harrow schoolboy and, later, as an army officer in India, he experimented with steam-driven engines for heavy road haulage. He left the army in 1876 and soon became a leading pioneer in electrical engineering, producing his own improved arc lamps, generators and other electrical plant at his Chelmsford work. His inventions covered the whole range of electrical equipment from hydro-electric installations to electric irons. He was also an expert on roads and road transport and contributed considerably to the design of military tanks in the first World War.

DENT, Arthur (d. 1607), Puritan vicar of South Shoebury from 1580, was the author of *The Plaine Man's Pathway to Heaven,* 'written dialogue-wise for the better understanding of the simple'. It was popular throughout the 17th and 18th centuries and ran into 41 editions.

DERHAM, William (1657-1735), vicar of Upminster from 1689, was an active member of a group within the Royal Society which included Newton, Wren, Ray, Flamsteed, and Hans Sloane. He was a close student of natural history and a voluminous writer on scientific and religious subjects. His letters to his friend, Dacre Barret of Belhus, show that his interests ranged from experiments in acoustics to observations on sun spots and the flight of ants.

FITZWALTER, Robert (d. 1235), Lord of Dunmow and Baynard's Castle, was one of the first barons to oppose King John's misgovernment. The barons elected him as their leader and 'Marshal of the army of God and Holy Church'. When John accepted Magna Carta at Runnymede on 15 June 1215, Fitzwalter was one of the 25 executors appointed to see that its terms were fully carried out. When John persuaded the Pope to annul the Charter and excommunicate the barons, Fitzwalter offered the Crown to Louis, son of King Philip of France. He was captured at the Battle of Lincoln, when Louis' forces were defeated, but was released in 1127. After fighting in the Fifth Crusade, he returned to England and made peace with the government of John's son, Henry III. He was buried before the high altar in Dunmow Priory.

FRY, Elizabeth (1780-1845), the daughter of John Gurney, Quaker and banker of Norwich, awakened Parliament and the nation to the appalling conditions in Newgate and other prisons. Her influence on prison reform spread throughout Europe, and she was received by the King of Prussia and King Louis-Philippe of France. She lived for 20 years at Plashet House, East Ham, and, later, at Upton Lane, and was buried in the Friends' cemetery at Barking. Among her friends and supporters were Sir Thomas

Elizabeth Fry

109

Thomas Fuller

Fowell Buxton (*q.v.*) and Elizabeth Hanbury, who lived in three centuries (1793-1901).

FULLER, Thomas (1608-61), author of *The Worthies of England,* spent about six years as vicar of Waltham. During this time, he completed Volume V of his *Church History of Britain,* dedicated to the Earl of Middlesex of Copt Hall, Epping, and wrote a *History of Waltham Abbey.*

GAUDEN, John (1605-62), Bishop of Worcester, was the son of the rector of Mayland. He is generally considered to be the author of *Eikon Basilike, the Pourtraicture of his Sacred Majestie in his Solitudes and Sufferings,* published at the time of Charles I's execution, when Gauden was Dean of Bocking.

GILBERT, William (1544-1603), physician to Queen Elizabeth and James I, was born at Colchester. He was the first man to study electricity, and, indeed, to use the word itself. His book on magnetism was warmly praised by the great Galileo. Gilbert was buried in Holy Trinity church, Colchester, where his monument, erected by his brothers, still stands.

GRAY, Charles (1696-1782), was educated at Colchester Royal Grammar School and Trinity College, Cambridge. When he married the widow of Ralph Creffield, they were given Colchester Castle and the adjacent house, The Hollytrees, as a wedding present. He became a prosperous barrister, an eminent antiquary, a friend of Philip Morant (*q.v.*), and M.P. for Colchester.

GRIFFIN, Sir John Griffin, fourth Lord Howard de Walden and first Lord Braybrooke (1719-97), was the son of William Whitwell of Oundle and was descended from the Lords Griffin of Braybrooke and from the Suffolk branch of the Howard family. He changed his name to Griffin in 1749. He fought in the War of Austrian Succession and the Seven Years' War, and left active service as a lieutenant-general and a Knight of the Bath; he was promoted to field-marshal in 1796. From 1749 to 1784 he was M.P. for Andover and was on close terms with Rockingham and Chatham. He became Lord-Lieutenant and Vice-Admiral of Essex. He inherited Audley End from his aunt, Lady Portsmouth, and thoroughly reorganised the estates. He restored the mansion, employing Robert Adam for much of the interior remodelling and Capability Brown for the layout of the environs.

110

GRIMSTON, Sir Harbottle, Baronet (1603-85), judge and Speaker of the Commons, was born at Bradfield Hall and was educated at Emmanuel College, Cambridge, and Lincoln's Inn. He was M.P. for Harwich and Recorder of the port before he became Recorder of Colchester, which he represented in the Short and Long Parliaments. He helped to frame the Grand Remonstrance and led the impeachment of Laud, whom he attacked violently. Generally, however, he was moderate in his views and left the country after the execution of Charles I. He was elected Speaker of the Convention Parliament in 1660, and was sent to Holland to recall Charles II.

HADDOCK, Nicholas (1686-1746), admiral and son of Sir Richard Haddock (*q.v.*), was the first to board the Spanish galleons at Vigo in 1702. He was present at the relief of Barcelona by Peterborough in 1706. At the battle of Cape Passaro, 1718, he led the van and contributed largely to Byng's great victory. He was made Commander-in-Chief at the Nore in 1733 and Admiral of the Blue in 1744. As he lay dying, he uttered those splendid words, often quoted, once by Nelson: 'My son, considering my rank in life and public affairs for so many years. I have left you but a small fortune, but it is honestly got and will wear well; there are no seamen's wages or provisions, not a single penny of dirt money in it'.

HADDOCK, Sir Richard (*c*. 1629-1715), admiral, was a distinguished member of that intrepid Leigh family which produced two admirals and at least seven captains in the century, *c*. 1650-*c*. 1750. He fought in the Second Dutch War. In the Third Dutch War, he commanded the *Royal James,* the Earl of Sandwich's flagship at the battle of Sole Bay, 1672, and miraculously escaped when the ship blew up. He survived those savage actions off the Dutch coast in the summer of 1673. He was knighted in 1675, and sat as M.P. for Shoreham, 1685-7. He was made Controller of the Navy in 1689, and was one of the joint Commanders-in-Chief of William III's expedition to Ireland. His moral audacity matched his physical courage—in 1709, his 80th year, he tried to screw compensation from the Admiralty for the loss of a toe at Sole Bay, 37 years earlier!

Sir Richard Haddock

HARRISON, William (1535-93), was rector of Radwinter from 1559. In his *Description of England*, 1577, he carefully notes the changes he remembers and gives a most valuable account of social life in Elizabethan times.

HARSNETT, Samuel (1561-1631), was born in Colchester and educated at Pembroke Hall, Cambridge. In 1587 he was appointed master of Colchester Grammar School, but in the following year he gave up this 'painful trade of teaching'. He became, successively, vicar of Chigwell, canon of St. Paul's, Archdeacon of Essex, Master of Pembroke Hall, Bishop of Chichester, Bishop of Norwich, and Archbishop of York. He founded Chigwell School and left his valuable library to Colchester Corporation. He is commemorated in Chigwell church by the finest 17th-century brass in the country.

HARVEY, Sir Eliab (1758-1830), admiral, K.G.C.B., was the son of William Harvey of Rolls Park, Chigwell, and great-great-nephew of William Harvey, the physician (*q.v.*). He commanded *The Fighting Temeraire* in 1803, and took part in the blockade of Brest. He fought at Trafalgar, and later served under both St. Vincent and Gambier in the Channel Fleet. His intemperate attack on Cochrane led to his dismissal in 1809, but he was reinstated in the following year. He had become M.P. for Maldon at the age of 21; for much of his later life he was one of the County Members.

HARVEY, Gabriel (*c.* 1545-1630), poet and scholar, was born and buried at Saffron Walden. While he was Fellow of Pembroke Hall, he became acquainted with Edmund Spenser. He was involved in a violent pamphlet war with the poets Robert Greene and Thomas Nash, a controversy now remembered mainly for Nash's pamphlet, *Have with you to Saffron Walden.*

HARVEY, William (1578-1657), chief physician to Charles I, and discoverer of the circulation of the blood, was educated at Cambridge and at the medical schools of Italy. In 1616, as lecturer at the College of Physicians, he first made public his views on the circulation of the blood, but it was not until 1628 that these were published in book form. When he died in London, the members of the College of Physicians followed his coffin to Hempstead in north-west Essex, where he is commemorated by an exceptionally fine bust.

William Harvey

HAWKWOOD, Sir John de (d. 1394), general and soldier of fortune, was the son of a tanner of Sible Hedingham. He served in the French wars of Edward III, and in 1359 he commanded a troop of free lances, who came to be known as the White Company.

LAYTONSTONE ACADEMY, ESSEX.

To the Gentlemen Educated at Mr. Emblin's School, this Plate is respectfully Dedicated by
Their Obliged Friend and Schoolfellow
Rob.t Sam.l Cull

28. Mr. Emblin's Academy at Leyton. Private schools flourished in the Georgian Age after the decline of the old grammar schools

29. Fairlop Fair, around the giant oak in Hainault Forest

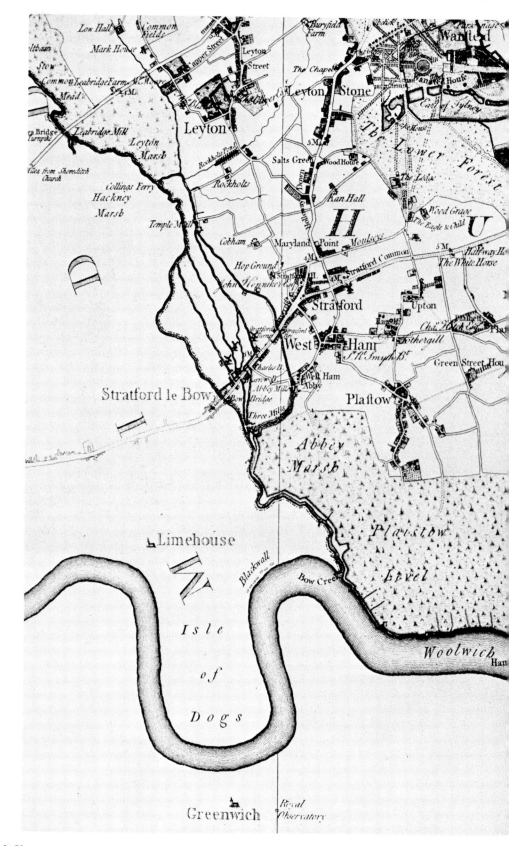

30. Part of Chapman and Andre's map of 1777, showing the extreme south-west corner of Essex before London began to spread over the border. In the north is Wanstead House in its imposing park; in the south, gibbets overlook the Thames; between, are the villages and small townships, now part of Greater London

31. Southend in 1831. By this time, the South End of Prittlewell was firmly established as a watering place o
fashion and reputation

32. The fishing port of Leigh-on-Sea, famous for its cockle boats

He led this well-equipped and well-disciplined force of 3,000 into Italy, where he served various Italian states, particularly Florence, with great distinction. He was buried in Florence cathedral, where a fresco by Paolo Ucello commemorates him. King Richard II obtained permission for his widow, a daughter of the Duke of Milan, to transfer his body to England. It is not known whether this was done or whether the monument to him in Sible Hedingham church is in fact merely a cenotaph.

The Armada Jewel

HENEAGE, Sir Thomas (d. 1595), Vice-Chamberlain to Queen Elizabeth I, was educated at the Queens' College, Cambridge. From 1553 to 1572, he represented Lincolnshire constituencies; in later parliaments, from 1585 until his death, he was M.P. for Essex. Elizabeth trusted him closely. She made grants of land to him, including the manor of Epping and the manor of Copt Hall, where he partially rebuilt the hunting lodge of the former abbots of Waltham. She also presented him with the famous Armada Jewel in the autumn of 1588.

HOPKINS, Matthew (d. 1647), of Manningtree, witchfinder, made journeys throughout the eastern counties to discover witches. In one year, 60 unfortunate women were hanged in Essex alone through his efforts. In 1646, he was exposed, and in the following year was hanged as a sorcerer.

HOWARD, Thomas, first earl of Suffolk and first Baron Howard de Walden (1561–1626), was the second son of the fourth Duke of Norfolk and grandson of Lord Audley (*q.v.*). As Lord Thomas Howard, he distinguished himself against the Armada and commanded the squadron off the Azores in 1591, when Sir Richard Grenville in the *Revenge* fought his memorable action against the Spaniards. He was appointed Lord Treasurer in 1614, when his vast mansion of Audley End, costing £200,000, was nearing completion. Five years later, he and his avaricious wife were imprisoned in the Tower for embezzlement. They were released on promising to pay a fine of £30,000. This, and his reckless extravagances, left him a ruined man.

HOLST, Gustav Theodore (1874–1934), studied composition under Stanford at the Royal College of Music. At first, he was influenced by the music of Grieg; then by Bach and Wagner, and, in later life, by English folk song and Tudor composers. In 1903, he gave up his career as a trombone player to write music. He became

William Derham

director of music at St. Paul's Girls' School, which for some years remained a welcome refuge for a diffident man who shunned fame and popularity. In 1914, he began his best-known work, *The Planets*, a suite for orchestra, and in 1920 he wrote his famous *Hymn of Jesus*. From 1917 to 1925 he lived at Thaxted near his friend, Conrad Noel, the Christian Socialist vicar of the town.

JOHN, Lewis (d. 1442), was the founder of the Fitzlewes family of West Horndon. About 1400, he emigrated from West Wales, possibly Carmarthenshire, to London, where he became a goldsmith and eventually a trusted financial adviser to the Lancastrian kings. He married Alice de Vere, daughter of the Earl of Oxford, in 1413, acquired the West Horndon estates and built West Horndon Hall. He became Sheriff of Essex and Herts. in 1416, and M.P. for Essex in 1420. His second wife was Anne, daughter of John Montagu, Earl of Salisbury.

JOHNSON, John (1732–1814), architect, born in Leicester, was established in London by 1766. He served as County Surveyor of Essex from 1782 to 1812. His public works include the elegant Moulsham Bridge over the Can and the Shire Hall, Chelmsford, with its large and particularly graceful County Room. Although he restored the nave of Chelmsford church (now the cathedral) in Gothic style, his major commissions are characterised by the use of the Neo-classical ornament introduced by Robert Adam. He designed a number of country houses in Essex, including Terling Place, Langford Grove (demolished), Bradwell Lodge, and Hatfield Place.

JOSSELIN, Ralph (1618–83), was born at Roxwell and was vicar of Earls Colne, 1641–83. He was a moderate Puritan who conformed after the Restoration of Charles II. His diary gives a valuable and illuminating account of a day-to-day life in north Essex and of the impact of national events on it.

LENNARD, Thomas, 17th Lord Dacre (1717–1786), was the posthumous only child of Richard Barret and his cousin, Lady Ann Lennard. In 1725 he inherited Belhus, Aveley, from his grandfather, Dacre Barret. Between 1745 and 1777 he transformed Belhus from a mainly 16th-century house into a Gothic edifice, which met with the approval of Horace Walpole. He became the 17th Lord Dacre in 1755 on the death of his mother. An antiquarian with a keen interest in family history, he reassembled the family portraits and gave support to Morant's *History of Essex.*

LISTER, Joseph, first Baron (1827–1912), was born in West Ham and educated at University College, London. He became professor of surgery at Glasgow University, but returned to London to spend the last 16 years of his working life at King's College. Influenced by the researches of Louis Pasteur, he introduced the use of antiseptics, which considerably reduced the number of deaths following operations and widened and revolutionised the practice of surgery. He received all the highest honours which the medical world could give, and was one of the original members of the Order of Merit.

John Locke

LOCKE, John (1632–1704), the great philosopher, author of *An Essay Concerning Toleration,* a treatise *On Education* and *An Essay Concerning Human Understanding,* spent the last 14 years of his with the Masham family at Otes, High Laver, and is buried in High Laver churchyard.

MANDEVILLE, Geoffrey de, first Earl of Essex (d. 1144), inherited the vast Essex estates granted to his grandfather by the Conqueror. He was also appointed Constable of the Tower by King Stephen. During the struggle for the throne between Stephen and the Empress Maud, he increased his power and possessions by deserting each rival in turn. After intriguing a second time with Maud, he was arrested by Stephen, deprived of the Tower and his Essex castles of Pleshey and Saffron Walden, and allowed to go free. It was said that he rushed from the king's presence 'like a vicious and riderless horse, kicking and biting'. He raised a rebellion in the Fens and was eventually killed fighting against Stephen at Burwell.

MARCONI, Guglielmo, Marchese (1874–1937), took out his first patent in 1896 for 'transmitting electrical impulses and signals'. In the following year he formed his Wireless Telegraph Company and established his first factory at Chelmsford in 1898. Here Marconi and his associates carried out most of the early research which enabled him in 1901 to hear in Newfoundland the first Morse messages sent across the Atlantic from his transmitting station in Cornwall. This achievement led immediately to the widening of wireless communication. Wireless equipment made at the Chelmsford works and constantly improved by the Marconi team

Sir Anthony Cooke

of scientists was fitted first to ships and then to aircraft. After the first World War, the Marconi Company, using its short-wave beam system, established a world-wide Imperial telegraph service. At Chelmsford, too, the first sound broadcast took place, when in June 1920 the voice of Dame Nellie Melba was heard in many countries.

MARSHALL, Stephen (*c.* 1594–1655), Puritan vicar of Finchingfield, was well known in the Wethersfield and Finchingfield area for his vehement preaching and saintly life. His greatest fame was gained nationally, when his preaching in London immediately before the Civil War affected the results of the elections to the Short Parliament and the important decisions of the Long Parliament in 1641.

MARTIN, Christopher (d. *c.* 1620), of Billericay, governor of the *Mayflower,* died soon after the landing of the Pilgrim Fathers at New Plymouth in the autumn of 1620.

MILDMAY, Sir Henry (d. *c.* 1664), of Wanstead, son of Sir Humphrey Mildmay of Danbury, was brought up at Court. He became Master of the King's Jewel House and M.P. for Maldon. He deserted Charles I in 1641, and became one of the judges at the king's trial in 1648–9, but did not sign the death warrant. At the Restoration, he was called to give account of the Crown jewels; he attempted to escape, was captured and sentenced to life imprisonment and to be drawn on a hurdle every year on 27 January (the day Charles was condemned to die) from the Tower to Tyburn gallows and back again.

MONCK, George, first Duke of Albemarle (1608–70), served Charles I in the Civil War and was captured by Fairfax in 1644. Later, he fought for parliament in Ireland. He became commander-in-chief in Scotland, and admiral in the First Dutch War, and, finally, commander-in-chief of all the parliamentary forces. At the end of 1659, after a period of confusion following Cromwell's death, he marched from Scotland to London, demanded the election of a new parliament and negotiated the Restoration of Charles II. He served in the Second Dutch War, and was largely responsible for its conduct. For the last 10 years of his life, he lived in great splendour at New Hall, Boreham, where he often entertained Charles II and his Court.

116

MORANT, Philip (1700–1770), eminent historian of Essex, became curate of Great Waltham in 1724, when Nicholas Tindal, the historian, was vicar. He held seven Essex livings at different times and was rector of both St. Mary-at-the-Walls, Colchester, and Aldham for the latter part of his life. His greatest work is the *History and Antiquities of the County of Essex,* published 1760–68.

Matthew Hopkins

MORRIS, William (1834–96), poet, artist, craftsman and Socialist, spent his first six years at Walthamstow. Later, he lived at Woodford Hall, adjoining Epping Forest. In those days, this fragment of the Forest of Essex had changed little since medieval times. It undoubtedly helped to form Morris's romantic desire to recover the lost colour, craftsmanship and simple life and ways of the Middle Ages. This is clearly seen in writings like *A Dream of John Ball* and *News from Nowhere,* in his edition of the works of Chaucer printed at his own Kelmscott Press, in his furniture and stained glass, and in his own, very English, form of Socialism.

NEVILLE, Richard Griffin, third Lord Braybrooke (1784–1858), was educated at Christ Church, Oxford, and Magdalene College, Cambridge. On succeeding his father in 1825, he moved to Audley End and made substantial alterations to the house, creating the imposing Library. He was the first editor of Pepys's *Diary* and the author of *The History of Audley End.*

OATES, Lawrence Edward Grace (1880–1912), joined Captain Robert Scott's Antarctic expedition, which reached the South Pole in January 1912, and was lost on the return journey. In the church at Gestingthorpe, his boyhood home, a brass plate 'in memory of a very gallant gentleman' records that 'when all were beset by hardship, he, being gravely injured, went out into the blizzard to die in the hope that by so doing he might enable his comrades to reach safety'.

OGLETHORPE, James Edward (1696–1785), soldier and philanthropist, obtained a charter in 1732 empowering him to settle undischarged debtors in a new colony in Georgia. He sailed with the first 120 settlers and spent many years organising the colony and securing its defences against the Spaniards in Florida. In 1743, he married Elizabeth, heiress of Sir Nathan Wright of Cranham Hall, which became his home for the rest of his life. He served under Cumberland during the Jacobite Rebellion of

1745. In later years, he was a well-known figure in London's literary and philanthropic circles and closely acquainted with Johnson, Boswell, Horace Walpole, Goldsmith, Burke and Hannah More.

PARKER, William, fourth Baron Monteagle and 11th Baron Morley (1575-1622), of Great Hallingbury, was closely related to the chief Roman Catholic families of the country. He became a Protestant in 1605, and in November of that year received a warning letter from his brother-in-law, Francis Tresham, which led to the detection of the Gunpowder Plot.

PENN, William (1644-1718), Quaker and founder of Pennsylvania, spent his early years at Wanstead, and went as a day boy to Chigwell School.

PETRE, Robert James, eighth Lord Petre (1713-42) was the posthumous son of Robert, the seventh Lord. He was undoubtedly a horticultural genius: a F.R.S. at 18, a friend of all leading naturalists and botanists, including Sir Hans Sloane, Peter Collinson, Linnaeus and John Bartram of Pennsylvania. During his short life Thorndon Hall became a centre of horticulture. His hothouses were the largest in the world—his Great Stove was 30ft. high and his Pinery, 60ft. long. He successfully replanted elms 60ft. high. He was a gifted landscape artist: the layout of Thorndon and Worksop were probably inspired by him. He married Anna Maria Barbara Radcliffe, daughter of the Jacobite third Earl of Derwentwater, executed in 1715. He began to rebuilt Thorndon Hall to the designs of Leoni, but this was halted by his untimely death.

Samuel Purchas

PETRE, Sir William (*c.* 1505-72), was one of the most gifted 'New Men' of the mid-Tudor age. An able lawyer, he served under Thomas Cromwell, became a skilled diplomatist and helped to dissolve the monasteries. He was Secretary of State to Henry VIII, Edward VI and Mary, and, as a valued elder statesman, he was consulted by Elizabeth and by her great minister, William Cecil, his friend and former colleague. He re-endowed and virtually refounded Exeter College, Oxford, his own college. He acquired large estates in mid-Essex, in his native county, Devon, and in other counties. He was the builder of Ingatestone Hall, still the family home, where he died in 1572. The Crown mason, Cornelius Cure, probably made his imposing monument in Ingatestone church.

PLUME, Thomas (1630-1704), Archdeacon of Rochester, was born in Maldon and educated at Chelmsford Grammar School and Christ's College, Cambridge. He was vicar of Greenwich from 1658 until his death. He was a noted preacher, but is mainly remembered for his benefactions: he founded the Plumian professorship of Astronomy at Cambridge, rebuilt Maldon Grammar School and left his valuable library to the borough of Maldon.

Francis Quarles

PURCHAS, Samuel (*c.* 1577-1626), was born at Thaxted and educated at Ṣt. John's College, Cambridge. He was curate of Purleigh, vicar of Eastwood in 1604 and, finally, rector of St. Martin's, Ludgate. He is famous for continuing the work of Hakluyt in collecting and editing the stories of voyages and travels made by men of his generation. He best-known collection is *Purchas his Pilgrimes,* published in 1625.

QUARLES, Francis (1592-1644), poet, was born at the family manor house of Stewards in the centre of Romford. He served as cup-bearer to James I's daughter, Elizabeth, the 'Queen of Hearts', on her marriage to the Elector Palatine. Later, he became private secretary to James Ussher, Archbishop of Armagh. By 1633 he was back again in Essex, at Roxwell, where he published his best-known poems, the *Emblems.*

RADCLIFFE, Thomas, third Earl of Sussex (1526-83), soldier and politician, was educated at Cambridge and became M.P. for Norfolk. He came into prominence for suppressing Wyatt's rebellion. He was Lord Deputy of Ireland from 1556 to 1564, where he governed vigorously but failed to subdue Shane O'Neill. He put down the Rising in the North, 1569, and drove the surviving rebels into Scotland. Elizabeth made him Lord Chamberlain and granted him New Hall, Boreham, formerly Henry VIII's summer palace of Beaulieu. His effigy and those of his father and grandfather lie together on one vast monument by Richard Stevens, the master of Epiphanius Evesham.

RAY, John (1627-1705), celebrated naturalist and founder of the modern study of botany, was the son of a Black Notley blacksmith. He was educated at Braintree Grammar School and Trinity College, Cambridge, and became university lecturer in Greek and mathematics. In 1658 he began his botanical tours of England and Wales with his friend and former pupil, Francis Willughby, and, four years later, they decided to compile a full

John Ray

and clear description of all animal and plant life. After Willughby's early death in 1672, Ray spent many years completing and editing his friend's work, notably the famous book on birds which appeared in 1676. He lived for two years at Faulkbourne Hall, the home of Edward Bullock. After his mother's death in 1679, he moved to Dewlands House, which he had built for her at Black Notley. His greatest work was his *History of Plants,* in three large volumes, completed just before his death.

REPTON, Humphry (1752-1818), landscape gardener, lived for his last 45 years in a cottage, later known as Repton's Cottage, at Hare Street, Romford. He lost his fortune in two business ventures, and then decided to be a landscape gardener, using the botanical knowledge he had acquired as a hobby. He became famous, and was employed by prominent landowners all over England. In Essex, he worked at Rivenhall Place, Highams (Walthamstow), Claybury Hall (Woodford), Stubbers (North Ockendon), and Woodford Hall.

RICH, Richard, first Baron (*c.* 1496-1567), founder of Felsted School, was a successful lawyer and politician. A Londoner, educated at Cambridge and the Middle Temple, he sat in the Commons as M.P., first for Colchester, then for Essex, 1529-48, and in the Lords, 1549-67, presiding as Lord Chancellor 1549-51. He was a Privy Councillor, 1536-59, and, as Chancellor of the new Court of Augmentations, 1536-44, supervised the disposal of monastic property. He was an efficient administrator, public and private; beginning with Leighs Priory, he bought scores of manors in Essex. His part as a young lawyer in the More and Fisher trials has antagonised historians. He died at Rochford Hall and was buried in Felsted church, where his grandson in 1621 erected the noble monument by Epiphanius Evesham.

RICH, Robert, second Earl of Warwick (1587-1658), the great-grandson of the first Lord Rich (*q.v.*), was educated at Emmanuel College, Cambridge. He was M.P. for Maldon before he succeeded to the earldom in 1619. In 1625 he became Lord Lieutenant of Essex, where he inherited widespread estates with seats at Rochford Hall and Leighs Priory. He helped to promote the settlement of the New England colonies at New Plymouth, Massachusetts and Connecticut. At home, he opposed the early measures of Charles I, became leader of the Puritan party, raised forces for Parliament at the outbreak of the Civil War, gained

120

33. (*right*) Chappel Viaduct on the Stour Valley Line is the most imposing Victorian monument in the county

34. (*below*) John Joseph Mechi took over Tiptree Hall in 1843 and turned it into a model of scientific farming

35.   Stansted Airport

36.   Work on the M11 Motorway

37. Broad Walk, Harlow

38. Bradwell nuclear generating station on its remote site near the tip of the Dengie peninsular

39. Modern sculptures in Lambourne church: the *Virgin and Child* and the *Risen Christ*, by the late T. B. Huxley-Jones

control of the fleet for Parliament and became Lord High Admiral. Working through gentlemen of similar Puritan views, notably Sir Thomas Barrington, he held Essex firmly on Parliament's side throughout the war.

ROE, Sir Thomas (c. 1581-1644), ambassador, was born at Low Leyton and educated at Magdalen College, Oxford. He was knighted by James I in 1605 and was popular at Court, especially with Henry, Prince of Wales, who persuaded him to explore the Amazon. In 1614, he was sent as ambassador to the court of the Mogul emperor, Jehangir, and secured improved trading conditions. Later, he was so successful as ambassador at Constantinople that the English merchants there were reluctant for him to return. When he did so, he brought back the *Codex Alexandrinus* copy of the Bible, and 29 manuscripts for the Bodleian. In 1629 he was sent on a mission to Gustavus Adolphus, King of Sweden, whom he persuaded to enter Germany as a champion of the Protestant cause in the Thirty Years' War. On his way back, he made trade treaties with Danzig and Denmark. He was famous for his personal charm, sound judgement and close knowledge of foreign affairs and British commerce. He was buried in Woodford parish churchyard.

ROUND, John Horace (1856-1928), historian and controversialist, was the son of John Round of West Bergholt and a member of the well-known family of Birch Hall. He was educated privately and at Balliol College, Oxford. He suffered from ill-health throughout his life; this may partly account for his readiness to rush into violent controversy with anyone from famous historians, like E. A. Freeman, to obscure genealogists. His scholarship was profound and formidable; his output was prodigious. He best-known books are his *Geoffrey de Mandeville,* 1892, and *Feudal England,* 1895, but his lasting fame may well lie in his work as founder of modern Domesday studies. To the *Victoria County Histories* he contributed 12 introductions to Domesday; his Essex introduction is a model essay, retaining all its original freshness.

Richard Rich,
Earl of Warwick

SMITH, Sir Thomas (1513-77), was born at Saffron Walden and was educated at Queens' College, Cambridge, and at Paris, Orleans and Padua. He returned to Cambridge and became Regius Professor of Civil Law and Vice-Chancellor. He entered the service of Protector Somerset, became one of the Secretaries of State, and was imprisoned for a time following the fall of Somerset. In

Charles Spurgeon

Elizabeth's reign, he became amabassador to France and, once again, Secretary of State. He rebuilt Hill Hall, Theydon Mount, and is buried beneath an elaborate tomb in the church nearby. His *De Republica Anglorum* gives an invaluable account of the structure of English government and society in his time.

SPURGEON, Charles Haddon (1843–92), son and grandson of Independent pastors, was born at Kelvedon. He became so powerful and popular as a Baptist preacher that Essex Hall in London was not large enough for his congregation. From 1861 he ministered at the Metropolitan Tabernacle, designed to hold 6,000 persons.

STRUTT, John William, third Baron Rayleigh (1842–1919), scientist, was the co-discoverer of argon. He was professor of experimental physics at Cambridge, 1879–84, and then retired to Terling Place, the family home, to continue his researches in his private laboratory. He was successively Fellow, Secretary, and President of the Royal Society. He became an original Member of the Order of Merit in 1902, Nobel prize-winner in 1904 and Chancellor of Cambridge University in 1908.

STRYPE, John (1643–1737), vicar of Leyton from 1669, was an important biographer and historian. His most famous works are his *Annals of the Reformation* and his *Lives* of Archbishops Cranmer, Parker, Grindal, and Whitgift, and of Sir Thomas Smith, the statesman (*q.v.*).

SYMONDS, Richard (1617-*c.*1692), Royalist and antiquary, was born at Black Notley. As a member of Charles I's lifeguard, he was present at Naseby and at other important battles in the Civil War. Between battles he filled his notebooks with accurate details of local antiquities, now of great value to local historians and antiquaries.

TALLIS, Thomas (*c.* 1510-85), composer, became organist at Waltham Abbey in 1540. He taught William Byrd (*q.v.*) and was known as the 'Father of English Church Music'. Some of his hymn-tunes, including 'Glory to Thee, my God, this night', are in general use, and his magnificent four-part Litany is often broadcast by the B.B.C.

TAYLOR, Isaac (1759–1829), engraver and writer for the young, was nonconformist pastor of Ongar and member of a talented family. His father, uncle, brother and son were all artists and engravers. His daughters, Jane (1783–1824) and Anne (1782–1866), wrote poems well known to thousands of children throughout the 19th century. It was Jane who wrote 'Twinkle, twinkle, little star'.

TURPIN, Richard (1706–39), highwayman, was the son of a Hempstead innkeeper. He joined the gang of ruffians based in Epping Forest, shot his partner, Tom King, by accident, and escaped to Yorkshire, where he was hanged for horse stealing at Knavesmire, York.

TUSSER, Thomas (*c.* 1524–80), agricultural poet, was born at Rivenhall and was educated at Eton and at King's College and Trinity Hall, Cambridge. He joined the Court as musician to Lord Paget. He failed as a practical farmer, but became famous for his poem, the 'Hundreth Good Points of Husbandrie', 1577, expanded later to 'Five Hundred Good Pointes'. This gives a full account of farming practices and the management of men, implements and animals. Many pithy, country proverbs can be traced back to Tusser's verse.

URSWYCK, Sir Thomas (d. 1479), lawyer and politician, became a rabid Yorkist. He was made Recorder of London in 1453 and was twice returned to Parliament for the City. In 1471, he was knighted and was appointed Chief Baron of the Exchequer in the following year. He was strongly suspected of complicity in the murder of Henry VI. He lived at Marks, Romford, a fortified manor house, demolished in 1808. He is considered to be largely responsible for reorganising the administration of the Liberty of Havering. On his brass at Dagenham he is shown in his judge's robes.

John Strype

VERE, Edward de, 17th Earl of Oxford (1550–1604), was born at Earls Colne. He became a favourite at Court and married Anne Cecil, daughter of Lord Burleigh, his former guardian. He was a judge at the trial of Mary, Queen of Scots, in 1586, and he fought against the Armada. He was patron of a company of players, known as 'The Earl of Oxford's Boys', who performed at Maldon and other places in Essex. Some people regard him as part-author of Shakespeare's plays.

VERE, John de, 13th Earl of Oxford (1443-1513), staunch Lancastrian, fought for Henry VI against Edward IV in the Wars of the Roses, and was imprisoned by the Yorkists for 10 years. He helped Henry VII to win the Crown at the Battle of Bosworth, 1485. Henry then restored to him his hereditary chamberlainship and made him Lord High Admiral and Constable of the Tower. In 1498 he entertained Henry at Castle Hedingham, his ancestral home. When the King saw the Earl's retainers drawn up to form a guard of honour, he said, 'My lord, I thank you for my good cheer, but I may not endure to have my laws broken in my sight. My attorney must speak with you'. After the King's departure he was fined £10,000 for breaking the laws against the keeping of armed retainers.

WASHINGTON, Lawrence (1602-52), Fellow of Brasenose College, Oxford, and rector of Purleigh, 1633-43, was buried in All Saints' churchyard, Maldon. He is generally considered to be the father of John Washington, who emigrated to Virginia and was the great-grandfather of George Washington, first President of the United States of America.

WILBYE, John (c. 1573-1638), of Colchester, was an accomplished composer of madrigals. In Colchester museum is a fine copy of his *First Set of English Madrigals,* 1599, including 'Flora gave me the fairest flower'.

WINSTANLEY, Henry (1644-1703), of Saffron Walden, engineer and engraver, was clerk of works to Charles II at Audley End. He designed the first Eddystone lighthouse and lost his life in the storm which destroyed it.

Index

Abberton 100
acts of parliament, 37-9, 53-5, 75, 78, 80-3, 85, 89, 93, 100, 102-3, 105, 107, 124
Adam, Robert 69, 110, 114
agriculture 12, 15, 31-2, 34, 36-40, 64, 68, 75-7, 79-80, 91, 94, 96-7, 102, 106, 123
Aldham 117
Alfred King 22
Alresford 92
Appleton, Sir Henry 94
architecture 12, 16, 18, 21-2, 25-8, 30, 40-5, 61-71 *passim*
Armada, Spanish 43
Ashdon 16, 23
Ashingdon 23
Assandune 23
Audley End 66, 69-70, 87, 113, 124
Audley,Thomas, Lord 51, 105, 110, 113, 117
Augustine, St. 20
Aulus Plautius 15
Aveley 75, 99, 114

Baddow, Great 37, 52, 72
Baddow, Little 11, 27, 54
Ball, John 38, 105, 117
Bardfield, Great 35, 55
Baring Gould, Sabine 105
Barking 47, 51, 67, 76-7, 82, 99, 103, 109
Barking Abbey 21, 25, 28-32, 51, 72
Barkingside 106
Barnardo, Thomas 105
Barnston 34
Barret, Dacre 75, 109, 114
Barret, Richard 75, 114
Barrington, Sir John 46
Barrington, Sir Thomas 57, 106, 121
Bartlow Hills 16
Basildon 32, 71, 102
Bastwick, John 106
Bate Dudley, Sir Henry 56, 106
Becontree 99
Bede, Venerable 21
Beeleigh Abbey 28, 30-1, 106
Belchamp Otton 22
Belgae 15
Bendlowes, William 44
Benfleet 22, 52
Bergholt, West 121
Beriff family 48
Bicnacre 50
Billericay 38, 46, 52-3, 56, 78, 116
Birch 70, 121
Birdbrook 37
Bishop's Stortford 87, 89, 92
Black Death 37
Blackmore 26, 29, 37
Blackwater, River 19, 35-6, 42-3, 88
Bobbingworth 52
Bocking 48, 110
Boreham 54-5, 58, 60, 69, 103, 116, 119

Boudicca, Queen 15, 18
Bourchier, Henry, Earl of Essex 28, 106
Bow Creek 94
Bowers Gifford 28
Bradfield 111
Bradwell-juxta-Mare 19, 20, 100, 106, 114; St. Peter's-on-the-Wall 21-2, 100
Braintree 29, 48, 50, 58, 72, 77, 79, 92, 119
Bramston, Sir John 107
Brentwood 36, 38, 46, 48, 58, 72-3, 89, 98, 107
Brightlingsea 47, 77, 91, 94
Brihtnoth 23, 42
Bromley, Great 27
Broomfield 20, 34
Broomway 14
Brown, 'Capability' 11, 69, 70, 110
Browne, Sir Anthony 72-3, 107
Buckhurst Hill 98
Bumpstead, Steeple 50, 67
Burnham-on-Crouch 54, 78, 99
Burstead, Great 46
Buxton, Sir Thomas Fowell 107, 110
Byrd, William, 67, 107, 122

Caesaromagus 18
Cam, River 18, 62, 69, 87
Camden, William 93-4
Campbell, Colen 69
Camulodunum 15
Can, River 18, 45-6
Canfield, Great 27, 37, 61
Canonium 18
Canvey Island 94, 98-9
Canute, King 23
Capel, Arthur, Lord 59
Cedd St. 19-21, 100
Charles I, King 57, 65, 106, 111-12, 116, 120, 122
Charles II, King 46, 53, 111, 114, 116, 124
Chappel 91
Chelmer, River 18, 36, 42-3, 45, 88
Chelmsford 29, 30, 37-8, 45-6, 55, 57, 70, 72, 79, 81, 88-9, 103, 107, 109, 113, 119. *See also* Moulsham
Chesterford, Great 18
Chignall Smealey 27, 34
Chigwell 70, 72-4, 103, 112, 118
Chingford 35, 99, 103
Chishall, Great 22
Chrishall 28
churches 18-23, 35-22 *passim*, 36, 40, 45, 48, 50-2, 54-6
Civil War 44, 53, 57, 116
Clacton 14, 79, 93, 95, 99
Claudius, Emperor 15
Clavering 61, 64
cloth industry 41, 43-6, 48, 50, 59, 64, 77, 79
Coggeshall 32, 38, 48, 54, 58, 64, 69, 72, 107

Colchester 16-19, 20-3, 30-1, 34, 38, 40-1, 43, 46-7, 50, 54-5, 57-61, 64, 69, 72-3, 77-8, 81-2, 85, 87, 89, 94, 99, 105-6, 110-12, 117, 120, 124
Colne, Earls 30, 54, 58, 73, 105, 107, 114, 123
Colne, River 15, 36, 40, 42, 87-7
Colne Valley 14, 90
Colonia Claudia Victricensis 15, 16, 18, 41
Constable, John 108
Cooke, Sir Anthony 108
Copford 27
Corringham 38
Coryton 98
Cranfield, Lionel, Earl of Middlesex 108
Cranham 117
Cressing 38, 68
Crompton, Col. R. Evelyn 108
Cromwell, Oliver 57, 59, 116
Croppenburg, Joas 94
Cunobelin 15

Daenningaes 20
Dagenham 82, 93, 98, 103, 123
Danbury 11, 20, 70, 116
Danelagh 22
Danes 22-3, 42
Deane, Sir Anthony 43
Debden 102
Dedham 57, 64, 69, 73, 108
Defoe, Daniel 43, 94
Dengie 11, 19-20, 43, 75
Dent, Arthur 109
Derham, William 56, 108
Domesday Book 22, 34-6, 40, 42, 121
Dunmow, Great 29, 45, 51-2, 54, 67, 109
Dunmow, Little 27, 29, 45
Durolitum 18
Dutch Wars 44, 111

Easton, Little 28, 106
Eastwood 119
Edmund Ironside, King 23
Edward the Confessor, King 23, 61, 65
Edward the Elder, King 22-3, 40, 42
Edward II, King 40
Edward III, King 28, 43, 46, 48, 61, 112
Edward IV, King 28, 106, 124
Edward VI, King, 51, 108, 118
Elizabeth I, Queen 43, 51-2, 55, 73, 78, 108, 110, 113, 118-19, 122
Epping 46, 53, 55, 58, 76, 81, 85, 108, 110, 113, 117, 123
Erkenwald, St. 21
Ermine Street 18
Eustace of Boulogne 34

Fairfax, Sir Thomas 57-9, 116
Fairlop 78
fairs, 40, 43, 45, 49, 78
Faulkbourne 62, 120
Feering 20
Felsted 64, 72-3, 97, 120
Finchingfield 11, 53, 67, 116
Fitzwalter, Robert, Lord of Dunmow 109
Fobbing 35, 38
Foulness 14
Frinton 93, 95, 98-9
Fry, Elizabeth 107, 109
Fuller, Thomas 110

Galleywood 78-9

Gauden, John 110
Gestingthorpe 117
Gidea Park 18, 98
Gilbert, William 110
Godwine, Earl 23
Gosfield 66, 77
Gray, Charles 42, 110
Greensted 22
Grey, Lady Catherine 67
Grey, Lady Jane 67
Griffin, Sir John, Lord Howard 69, 87, 110
Grimston, Sir Harbottle 111
Guthrum, King 22

Haddock family 47, 111
Haddock Nicholas 111
Haddock, Sir Richard 111
Hadleigh 19, 21, 25, 61, 108
Hadstock 23
Hainault 76, 99
Halstead 40, 48, 54, 58, 73
Ham, East 76-7, 82, 97, 99, 103, 109. See also Newham
Ham, West 51, 71, 76-7, 79, 82-3, 94, 97, 100, 103, 115. See also Newham
Hanningfield, West 27, 100
Harlow 46, 55, 71, 85, 98, 102
Harold Hill 99
Harold, King 23
Harrison, William 111
Harsnett, Samuel, Archbishop 73, 112
Harvey, Sir Eliab 112
Harvey, Gabriel 112
Harvey, William 112
Harwich 43-4, 69, 78, 81-2, 91, 94, 111
Hasten 22
Hastings, Battle of 23, 34
Hatfield Broad Oak 29, 50, 106
Hatfield Peverel 29, 114
Havering-at-Bower 20, 48, 65, 123
Hawkwood, Sir John 112
Hedingham, Castle 36, 39, 61, 77-8, 86, 124
Hedingham, Sible 78, 112-3
Hempstead 112, 123
Heneage, Sir Thomas 113
Henry II, King 40
Henry VI, King 124
Henry VII, King 61, 124
Henry VIII, King 50-1, 105, 118-19
Heybridge 88
Holst, Gustav 113
Honywood, Sir Thomas 58
Hopkins, Matthew 113
Hopper, Thomas 70
Horham Hall 64
Horkesley, Little 28
Hornchurch 48, 52, 82, 102-3
Horndon, East 20, 27
Horndon, West (Thorndon) 62, 68-9, 107, 114, 118
Howard, Thomas, Earl of Suffolk 113
Hullbridge 14

Iceni 16
Ilford 29, 76-7, 82, 103
Ingatestone 22, 25, 27, 49, 51, 66-7, 70, 85, 118
Ingrave 99

James I, King 43, 108, 110, 119, 121
Jaywick 94, 99
John, Lewis 62, 114

Johnson, John 69, 106, 114
Josselin, Ralph 54, 58, 114
Julius Caesar 15

Kelvedon 18, 122
Kelvedon Hatch 70
Knight, Thomas 76
Knights of St. John 25

Langdon Hills 11
Langford 114
Langham 54, 108
Langley 11
Latton 28-9, 50, 57
Laud, William, Archbishop 52, 111
Laver, High 115
Lawford 27, 69
Layer Marney 52, 66
Layfield, Edmund 52
Lea, River 14, 22, 35, 77, 87, 93, 97
Leighs, Great and Little, 34, 58, 66, 120
Leigh-on-Sea 47, 94, 111
Lennard, Thomas, Lord Dacre 114
Leoni, Giacomo 69, 118
Lexden 58
Leyton 77, 82, 103, 121-2
Leytonstone 77, 97
Lisle, Sir George 59
Lister, Joseph, Lord 115
Locke, John 115
London 16, 18, 20-2, 31, 34, 46-8, 58, 70,
    73, 76-9, 82, 86, 89-91, 94-103, 114-16,
    123
Loughton 70, 98
Lucas, Sir Charles 57-9

Maldon 11, 22-3, 29, 34, 40, 42-3, 47, 55,
    72, 81-2, 88, 91, 94, 107, 112, 119, 120,
    123-4
Mandeville, Geoffrey de 34, 44, 115, 121
Manningtree 47, 87, 94, 113
Marconi, Guglielmo, Marchese 115
Margaretting 20, 27
markets 15, 40, 43-6, 48
Marshall, Stephen 53, 116
Martin, Christopher 116
Mary Tudor, Queen 51-2, 107-8, 118
Mashbury 34
Matching 27, 68
Mayland 110
Mechi, J. Joseph 96
Mellitus 20
Mercia 23
Mersea 22, 58, 94
Mersea, East 22, 105
Mildmay, Benjamin, Earl Fitzwalter 43, 69,
    77
Mildmay, Sir Henry 116
mills 35-6
Mistley 47, 89, 94
monasteries 20, 25, 29-32, 50, 72
Monck, George, Duke of Albemarle 116
Monoux, Sir George 73
Morant, Philip 56, 110, 117
Morris, William 117
Moulsham 15, 18, 45, 69, 77, 79, 114
Mountnessing 85
Moze 38
Mucking 20

Navestock 27
Nazeing 76

Nesfield, Eden 70
Neville, Richard, Lord Braybrooke 117
Newham 35, 52. See also Ham, East, and
    Ham, West
Newport 62, 73-4
Noel, Conrad 114
Norden, John 13
Norman Conquest 22-3, 27, 34, 36, 61
Normans 23, 25, 27, 29, 36, 40, 42, 46, 61,
    65, 70, 86
Northey 23
North Sea 11, 19, 93
Norwich, George, Lord 57-9
Notley, Black 64, 119, 120, 122

Oates, Lawrence 117
Ockendon, North 52, 120
Odo, Bishop of Bayeux 34
Oglethorpe, James 117
Olaf Tryggvason 23
Ongar, Chipping 61, 85, 123
Orsett 16
Osyth, St. 21-2, 27, 30-1, 64
Othona 19, 21

Paglesham 94
Paine, James 65
Palladio, Andrea 68
Panfield 66
Parker, William, Lord Monteagle 118
Payne, John 55
Peasants' Revolt 37-9
Pebmarsh 28
Penn, William 118
Pentlow 27
Petre, John, Lord 107
Petre, Robert Edward, Lord 55, 68-9
Petre, Robert James, Lord, 118
Petre, Sir William 51, 66-7, 118
Pilgrim Fathers 116
Pitsea 91
Plaistow 76-7
Plantagenet, Isabella, Countess of Essex 28
Pleshey 34, 36, 61, 115
Plume, Thomas 119
Prittlewell 20, 31, 77, 94-5
Purchas, Samuel 119
Purfleet 77, 86, 98
Purleigh 119, 124

Quarles, Francis 119

Radcliffe, Thomas, Earl of Sussex 119
Radwinter 111
railways 42-5, 47, 86, 88-92
Ray, John 119
Rayleigh 36, 46, 61
Reformation 45, 50-2, 56
Rennie, John 88
Repton, Humphry 70, 120
Rich, Richard, Lord 72, 120
Rich, Robert, Earl of Warwick 57-8, 120
Richard II, King 38, 61, 106, 113
Rivenhall 18, 70, 120, 123
roads 18, 42-3, 45-6, 48, 58, 71, 76-8,
    85-8
Rochford 27, 47, 66, 94, 102, 120
Rochford Hundred 14, 78
Roding, River 88
Roe, Sir Thomas, 121
Rolf, Thomas 39
Roman River 15

127

Romans 11, 12, 15-19, 26, 34, 40-1, 47, 85, 93
Rome 20
Romford 22, 48, 70, 82, 85, 91, 98, 103, 108, 119-20, 123
Roothings, The 20, 34
    Abbess R. 22, 107
    Aythorpe R. 25
    Beauchamp R. 21
Roses, Wars of 39
Round, J. Horace 121
Roxwell 107, 114, 119

Saling, Little 54
Sandon 27, 29
Saxons 19-22, 34, 36, 40, 42-3, 45-7, 61, 85
schools 51, 54-5, 67, 72-4
Shaw, Norman 70
Shell Haven 98
Shenfield 85, 99
Sherrin, George 70
Shoebury, South 109
Smith, Sir Thomas 121-1
Southchurch 14
Southend-on-Sea 47, 67, 77, 82, 89, 91, 95, 98-9, 103
Southminster 35
Springfield 35, 58
Spurgeon, Charles 122
Stane Street 18, 45, 92
Stanford-le-Hope 38
Stanway 21
Stebbing 27, 55
Steeple 96
Stephen, King 68
Stifford 77
Stock 26
Stondon Massey 107
Stort, River 87, 93
Stour, River 43, 47, 87, 91, 93
Stratford 51, 77, 90
Strutt, John William, Lord Rayleigh 122
Strype, John 58, 122
Suetonius Paulinus 16
Symonds, Richard 122

Tallis, Thomas 107, 122
Taylor, Isaac 123
Tendring 14, 22
Terling 34, 69, 114, 122
Tey, Great 78
Thames Haven 90, 98
Thames, River 11, 14, 22, 35, 43, 79, 87-8, 93, 98
Thaxted 25, 36-7, 44, 64, 114, 119
Theydon Mount 66, 122
Thoby Priory 31
Thorndon. *See* Horndon, West

Thorpe-le-Soken 22
Thremhall Priory 31
Thundersley 20
Thurrock, Little 16
Tilbury 20, 58, 90, 93, 98-9
Tilty 31-2
Tiptree 32, 96
towns 16, 18, 34, 36-7, 40-49 *passim*
Tovi 23
Trinovantes 14, 15
Turpin, Richard 123
Tusser, Thomas 123
Tyler Wat 38

Upminster 64, 99, 109
Urswyck, Sir Thomas 123

Vanbrugh, Sir John 69
Vere family 61
Vere, Edward de, Earl of Oxford 123
Vere, John de, Earl of Oxford 124

Wakering, Great 14
Walden, Saffron 28-9, 31-2, 36, 40, 43-4, 51, 57, 61-2, 64, 69, 72-4, 77, 105, 112, 115, 121, 124
Walker family 45, 63, 68
Walpole, Horace 70, 114, 118
Waltham Abbey 23, 29, 30, 32, 35, 38, 46, 77, 79, 110, 113, 122
Waltham, Great 3, 64, 117
Walthamstow 70, 82, 93, 97, 103, 117, 120
Walton-on-the-Naze 14, 77, 89, 95, 99
Wanstead 35, 68-9, 103, 116, 118
Washington, Lawrence 124
Watling Street 22
Weald, North 102
Weald, South 49, 107
Wedmore, Treaty of 22
Wesley, John 55
Western, Charles, Lord 75
Wethersfield 38
Widdington 20, 62
William I, King 34
William III, King 111
Wimbish 28, 64
Winstanley, Henry 124
Witham 22, 46, 50, 69, 78, 91
Wivenhoe 38, 62, 70, 78, 87, 108
Wolsey, Thomas, Cardinal 50
Woodford 79, 80, 82, 98, 103, 117, 120-1
Woods, Richard 70
Wormingford 35
Wren, Sir Christopher 88
Writtle 29, 32, 45, 106
Wilbye, John 124

Young, Arthur 76, 97